# north carolina

# afield

A GUIDE TO NATURE CONSERVANCY PROJECTS IN NORTH CAROLINA

The Nature Conservancy

Protecting nature. Preserving life.™

overleaf: Penny's Bend (Jodie LaPoint); this page: Albemarle Sound (John Warner)

# north carolina

# afield

## A GUIDE TO NATURE CONSERVANCY PROJECTS IN NORTH CAROLINA
### 2ND EDITION

By Ida Phillips
Edited by Maura High
The Nature Conservancy, North Carolina Chapter
Durham, North Carolina

By Ida Phillips

Edited by Maura High

2nd edition revised and updated by Scott Belan, Debbie Crane, Margaret Fields, and Maria Sadowski

Cover photo: Big Yellow by John Warner

Design by 8 Dot Graphics

Published by

The Nature Conservancy, North Carolina Chapter

4705 University Drive, Suite 290

Durham, NC 27707

(919) 403-8558

4 3 2 1

ISBN 978-0-9675026-2-5

Library of Congress Control Number 2008924665

(Marge Limbert)

THE NORTH CAROLINA CHAPTER OF THE NATURE CONSERVANCY CELEBRATED ITS 30TH ANNIVERSARY IN 2007. In 1977, the Conservancy had protected 40,692 acres. Today, that acreage has grown to nearly 700,000, and the Conservancy is working daily to add to the special places it protects within North Carolina's borders.

None of our work would be possible without our conservation partners—federal, state, and local government; land conservancies; corporations; businesses; and people like you, who love and appreciate this beautiful state. We can't do it alone, but together we can preserve our natural heritage.

Take the time to thumb through *North Carolina Afield*. If you don't know it already, you'll find that North Carolina is a pretty special place from its mountains to its coast. The Nature Conservancy is committed to ensuring that remains the case. If you're not already one of our conservation partners, I hope you'll become one.

Katherine D. Skinner

*Executive Director*
*The Nature Conservancy, North Carolina Chapter*

# table of contents

Big Yellow Mountain (Christina Cheatham)

New River Headwaters (John Warner)

Chowan River (Debbie Crane)

## How We Work

THE NATURE CONSERVANCY'S MISSION IS TO PRESERVE THE PLANTS, ANIMALS, AND NATURAL COMMUNITIES THAT REPRESENT THE DIVERSITY OF LIFE ON EARTH BY PROTECTING THE LANDS AND WATERS THEY NEED TO SURVIVE.

The Conservancy uses a strategic, science-based approach to identify high-priority areas for conservation. The Conservancy doesn't focus on protecting a particular species; it concentrates on protecting entire landscapes and restoring the natural processes such as water flow or fire that sustain ecosystems. This field guide details a number of those North Carolina landscapes, from the Blue Ridge Escarpment in western North Carolina to the Onslow Bight on the Coastal Plain.

Recent major Nature Conservancy accomplishments in North Carolina are ensuring the survival of unusual plant species such as Gray's lily in the west and Venus flytrap in coastal swamps, rare animals such as mountain bog turtles or red-cockaded woodpeckers in the Sandhills, and special habitats such as mountain cranberry bogs or peat pocosins.

The Nature Conservancy is the largest conservation organization in the world, working in all 50 states and more than 30 countries. It has seven priority conservation initiatives—forests, protected areas, freshwater, marine, invasive species, fire, and climate change. To date, the Conservancy has

(The Nature Conservancy)

protected more than 117 million acres around the world, including almost 700,000 acres in North Carolina.

The Conservancy approaches conservation challenges in a nonconfrontational way, looking for a pragmatic solution. It recognizes that no single organization can solve a conservation problem; solutions are community-based and community-driven. It acknowledges that in order for conservation to succeed, stakeholders must believe in and support the conservation approach.

In order to pursue a landscape-based approach to conservation in North Carolina, the Conservancy has established six offices across the state. The newest, the Northern Mountains Office in Boone, opened in summer 2008 in recognition of the need to focus on preservation in the northwestern corner of the state. Other offices are located in Asheville, Wilmington, Halifax, Southern Pines, and Nags Head. Contact information for those landscape offices is available on page 7.

Recent major North Carolina Conservancy accomplishments include the protection of 76,563 acres in four distinct landscapes—the Roanoke, Upper Tar, and Chowan Rivers in northeastern North Carolina, and Juniper Creek in the state's far southeastern tip—and protection of the entire Alligator River shoreline in northeastern North Carolina.

The 76,563-acre acquisition was part of the single largest private conservation sale in the history of the South. In 2006, International Paper sold nearly 220,000 acres of forestland across 10 states to The Nature Conservancy and the Conservation Fund. Most of the North Carolina land was bought by The Nature Conservancy and transferred to the North Carolina Wildlife Resources Commission, adding tens of thousands of acres to the state's game land program and opening these lands and waters to hunting, fishing, hiking, boating, and other recreational uses. With this deal, 300 river and stream miles were protected, including valuable habitat and spawning grounds for a number of freshwater mussels and fishes.

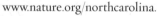

sheep laurel (Mark Daniels)

In spring 2008, The Nature Conservancy celebrated the transfer of the final 9,000 acres of land along the Alligator River to the Wildlife Resources Commission, making the Alligator the first North Carolina river to have its shoreline totally protected. That final deal builds on an effort that began with an 118,000-acre gift to the Conservancy back in 1984. Today, more than half a million acres have been protected in the far northeastern corner of North Carolina thanks to the efforts of the Conservancy and its many conservation partners.

## How You Can Become Involved

A private, nonprofit organization, The Nature Conservancy is rooted in a strong membership base. More than a million Americans are Conservancy members, including over 21,000 North Carolinians. In addition to an individual membership, you can support the conservation through estate-planning as a member of the Legacy Club. You or your business can also contribute to specific conservation activities across the state or globally. To find out more about the North Carolina Chapter, you can call (919) 403-8558 or check our web site at www.nature.org/northcarolina.

## Using the *North Carolina Afield* Guidebook

This book provides information about a number of natural areas The Nature Conservancy has helped to protect. It doesn't include every piece of property protected with Conservancy intervention, but includes a good representation of important North Carolina landscapes.

Much of that land has been transferred to public ownership. Those lands include state and federal parks, state and federal forests, federal wildlife refuges, state marine/estuarine reserves, and state game lands. Each of those entities has rules and regulations about visits, but for the most part they are open year-round. Some of the most important

Pyxie-moss (The Nature Conservancy); Waterlillies (Ida Phillips)

conservation areas have been transferred to the N.C. Division of Wildlife Resources Commission for inclusion in state game lands. The Commission maintains game lands as multiuse conservation areas and welcomes nonhunters as visitors. All game land visitors should check on hunting schedules prior to their visits and be prepared. That information is available on the web at www.ncwildlife.org or by calling 1 (800) 662-7137. Hunting is also allowed at national wildlife refuges; you can check on refuge hunting schedules on www.fws.gov/refuges.

Earlier editions of this guidebook relied heavily on written directions. This version refers visitors to sources that weren't readily available just a few years ago. Many of the public agencies represented in this guidebook maintain excellent web sites, which provide directions or downloadable maps. Visitors can also consult other online tools for directions. A good source for topographical maps is the North Carolina Geological Survey at www. geology.enr.state.nc.us or (919) 733-2423.

A few of The Nature Conservancy preserves are readily accessible to all visitors

Monarch butterfly (John Warner)

and are open year-round. But most Nature Conservancy preserves are only accessible through Conservancy-conducted field trips. The reason for this is that these preserves contain special plants, animals, or habitats that could be easily disturbed or irreparably damaged by visitors hiking in the wrong place.

No matter which place you decide to visit, please make sure to follow the appropriate visitor rules. They vary from place to place, so familiarize yourself with the requirements before you leave home. Remember, these are special landscapes. That means following good etiquette in the wild. Some things are universal. Never feed, touch, or scare wildlife—even if that cute animal looks as if it needs your

assistance. Always carry out what you carry in and make up for the lapses of others by carrying out litter you find along the way.

The Nature Conservancy is particularly concerned with preventing invasive plants and animals from spreading. We can all slow the spread of these invasives by taking a few simple steps. Before you visit a natural area, brush off your pant legs and check for seeds that can become established in new areas. If you have a choice between walking and driving through an area, remember that walking greatly reduces the risk of spreading invasives. Aquatic invasive species may attach themselves to boats, so you should always clean your boat before moving it from one body of water to another. Another problem is nasty creatures that hitchhike on firewood you might bring for a campfire. Always use locally acquired firewood; never bring firewood with you. You don't want to be the unwitting person who spreads a bug that could kill the very beauty you are visiting.

Many of the trips detailed in this guidebook are best made by boat. Boat rentals are uncommon in some parts of the state, so plan ahead and bring your own. Before you embark on a paddling trip, find out about current river or stream conditions. With the Internet, that information is just a few clicks away. Many of the public land managers also post information on their web sites about ongoing hazards like high water, fire, or closures of particular areas.

Finally, the landscapes detailed in this guidebook are special because they are wild and undeveloped. Trails may be primitive or nonexistent. There will also be natural hazards such as cliffs and ravines, poisonous insects, reptiles, and plants. North Carolina has its share of diseases that are contracted outside. Mosquito-borne illnesses like West

Raccoon (Bill Lea)

Nile virus or Eastern equine encephalitis and tick-borne illnesses like Rocky Mountain spotted fever or Lyme disease can be acquired in a walk through the woods. Always prepare for the environment you're visiting; that means wearing proper clothes and shoes, using insect repellent where appropriate, and carrying water or other provisions. Some of the hikes described in this guidebook are for people who are physically fit; if you're out of shape, don't attempt them. This is not meant to scare you, but to remind you to use common sense when in the wild.

Enjoy *North Carolina Afield*. Even if you are only an armchair visitor, you'll learn a lot about some of North Carolina's most special landscapes. Though the places described in this book are wonderful, we still have work to do. Special landscapes remain unprotected, and The Nature Conservancy is working tirelessly to conserve these areas before they disappear. We hope that reading this book will encourage you to join our efforts, if you haven't already done so. Together, we can add to the entries in future editions of this guidebook.

Alligator River (John Warner)

If you have any type of inquiry for the North Carolina Chapter, including questions about membership, planned giving, or natural area protection, contact:

**The Nature Conservancy**
**North Carolina Chapter Office**
4705 University Drive, Suite 290
Durham, NC 27707
(919) 403-8558
northcarolina@tnc.org
www.nature.org/northcarolina

### District Offices

**North Carolina Mountains Office**
P.O. Box 17519
Asheville, NC 28816
(828) 350-1431

**Northern Mountains Office**
P.O. Box 92
Boone, NC 28607
(828) 268-9551

**Roanoke River Office**
P.O. Box 327
Halifax, NC 27839
(252) 578-4115

**Nags Head Woods Ecological Preserve**
701 West Ocean Acres Drive
Kill Devil Hills, NC 27948
(252) 441-2525

**Southeastern Coastal Plain Office**
131 Racine Drive, Suite 101
Box Number 5
Wilmington, NC 28403
(910) 395-5000

**Sandhills Project Office**
P.O. Box 206
Southern Pines, NC 28388
(910) 246-0300

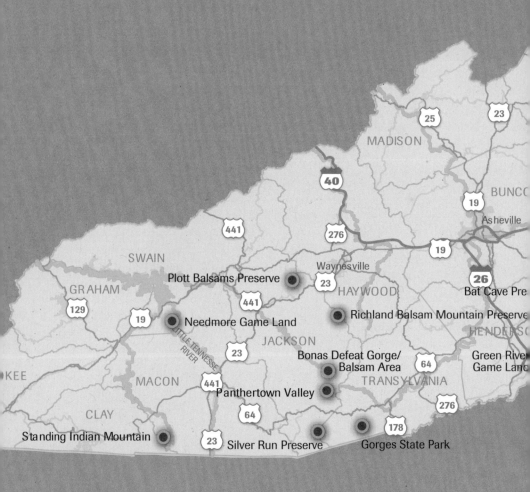

25

23

MADISON

40

BUNC

19

441

276

Asheville

19

SWAIN

Waynesville

26

Plott Balsams Preserve

23

HAYWOOD

Bat Cave Pre

GRAHAM

441

129

19

Needmore Game Land

Richland Balsam Mountain Preserve

HENDERSO

LITTLE TENNESSEE RIVER

JACKSON

441

23

Bonas Defeat Gorge/
Balsam Area

64

Green Rive
Game Land

KEE

MACON

441

Panthertown Valley

TRANSYLVANIA

CLAY

64

276

Standing Indian Mountain

23

Silver Run Preserve

178

Gorges State Park

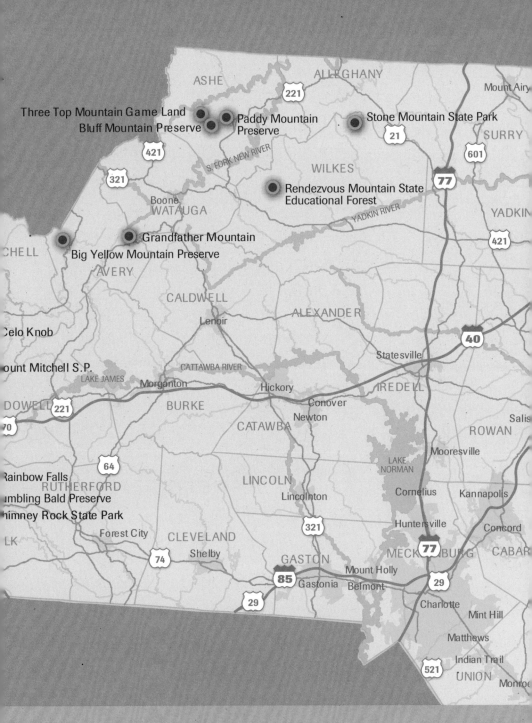

Three Top Mountain Game Land
Bluff Mountain Preserve

Paddy Mountain
Preserve

Stone Mountain State Park

Rendezvous Mountain State
Educational Forest

Grandfather Mountain

Big Yellow Mountain Preserve

Celo Knob

Mount Mitchell S.P.

Rainbow Falls
Rumbling Bald Preserve
Chimney Rock State Park

ASHE
ALLEGHANY
Mount Airy
SURRY
S. FORK NEW RIVER
WILKES
Boone
WATAUGA
YADKIN RIVER
YADKIN
AVERY
CHELL
CALDWELL
Lenoir
ALEXANDER
Statesville
CATTAWBA RIVER
LAKE JAMES
Morganton
Hickory
IREDELL
DOWELL
BURKE
Conover
Newton
CATAWBA
ROWAN
Mooresville
LAKE
NORMAN
LINCOLN
Cornelius
Kannapolis
Lincolnton
Huntersville
Concord
Forest City
RUTHERFORD
CLEVELAND
MECKLENBURG
CABAR
LK
Shelby
GASTON
Mount Holly
Charlotte
Gastonia
Belmont
Mint Hill
Matthews
Indian Trail
UNION
Monroe
Salis

Big Yellow Mountain Preserve (John Warner)

(John Warner)

Tʜᴇ Sᴏᴜᴛʜᴇʀɴ Aᴘᴘᴀʟᴀᴄʜɪᴀɴ Mᴏᴜɴᴛᴀɪɴs ᴅᴏᴍɪɴᴀᴛᴇ ᴛʜᴇ ᴡᴇsᴛᴇʀɴ ᴛʜɪʀᴅ ᴏꜰ Nᴏʀᴛʜ Cᴀʀᴏʟɪɴᴀ, ᴘᴀʀᴛ ᴏꜰ ᴀ ᴄʜᴀɪɴ ᴏꜰ ᴀɴᴄɪᴇɴᴛ ᴘᴇᴀᴋs ᴀɴᴅ ᴠᴀʟʟᴇʏs sᴛʀᴇᴛᴄʜɪɴɢ ᴍᴏʀᴇ ᴛʜᴀɴ 1,500 ᴍɪʟᴇs ꜰʀᴏᴍ Cᴀɴᴀᴅᴀ ᴛᴏ ᴄᴇɴᴛʀᴀʟ Aʟᴀʙᴀᴍᴀ. The Nature Conservancy has worked to protect the tremendous natural diversity of the Southern Appalachians in North Carolina for more than 30 years, and some of the Conservancy's most important current projects can be found here.

The towering mountain peaks, rock outcrops, and waterfalls that characterize the Southern Appalachians create many specialized habitats and unique natural communities. This is a region of extremes, featuring both the oldest river in North America (the New River) and the highest peak east of the Mississippi River (Mount Mitchell).

From bog turtles to black bears, peregrine falcons to ruffed grouse, the Southern Appalachians are home to a wide array of species. Steep mountainsides nurture a profusion of wildflowers, fissure caves provide habitat for endangered bats and rare salamanders, and large forest blocks host vast numbers of migrating songbirds.

The Conservancy has helped preserve some of the most iconic natural landmarks in the Southern Appalachians—places such as Grandfather Mountain, the Jocassee Gorges, and the Roan Highlands. Conservancy preserves at Bluff Mountain and Bat Cave are among our oldest projects in the state, and new efforts are under way to establish state parks and protected natural areas across the region. The Conservancy counts as its partners in the Southern Appalachians conservation-minded local landowners, a range of state agencies, and a strong, active land trust community.

New River Headwaters (John Warner)

THE NEW RIVER HEADWATERS AREA RANKS AS ONE OF THE MOST DIVERSE AND CRITICALLY important biological hotspots in the entire Southern Appalachians.

Many species found here came to the region just one step ahead of the encroaching Ice Age and remained in the high peaks of these rugged mountains after the ice receded 10,000 years ago.

The New River Headwaters are home to many rare plants, including the world's largest population of federally endangered Heller's blazing star.

The landscape of mountain bogs and boulderfield forests is rich with unusual natural communities and endangered plants and animals. It faces the dual threats of rapid development and habitat fragmentation.

New River Headwaters (John Warner)

**Ashe County • 2,087 acres**

## Features

A walk around Bluff Mountain offers scenic beauty, unusual landforms, and extraordinary botanical variety. Although relatively small in size, Bluff is one of the most ecologically significant natural areas in the Southeast. Hiking on Bluff, in just a few dozen steps you can walk from a Carolina hemlock forest to a dwarf red oak—white oak forest to a rare flat-rock plant community. A broad, high plateau containing an unusual wetland, a southern Appalachian fen, adds to Bluff's unique character.

Bluff Mountain lies in the Blue Ridge division of the Appalachian Mountain Range in Ashe County. It is part of a local mountain chain that includes Three Top (in this guide) and Phoenix Mountains and that is characterized by a substrate of mineral-rich rock called hornblende gneiss. The gneiss is unusually rich in minerals such as calcium and potassium that provide important nutrients for plants.

A fertile home for over 400 species of plants, including Indian paintbrush, Gray's lily, fringed gentian, spreading avens, and sundew, Bluff Mountain is known for a changing floral show from April through October that includes 25 endangered, rare, or threatened flowering plant species. The high-elevation hardwood forests of Bluff provide ideal nesting habitat for many neotropical migratory bird species such as black-throated green warbler, veery, rose-breasted grosbeak, scarlet tanager, and blue-headed vireo. During field trips in the spring, you may hear the distinctive drumming of ruffed grouse. Elusive bobcats den in the shelter of rocky outcrops, while ravens are often seen soaring over the cliffs.

## Conservation Highlights

Bluff Mountain's inaccessibility has protected it from major disturbances. Shortly after the North Carolina Chapter office opened in 1977, the staff began working with the mountain's owners, the Wyn Edwards and Mac Edwards families of West Jefferson, to explore a way to protect the fragile area for conservation. The Nature Conservancy purchased 701 acres of Bluff from the Edwards family in 1978. The chapter continues to work to protect this entire natural area, having expanded the preserve as recently as 2007.

## Trip Planner

This Nature Conservancy preserve is accessible through a locally based ecotourist guide, Doug Munroe. Contact Doug at (336) 385-6507, Monday to Friday from 7 a.m. to 6 p.m., to schedule a trip to this site.

## Ownership/Access

The Nature Conservancy
P.O. Box 17519
Asheville, NC 28816
(828) 350-1431
www.nature.org/northcarolina

Lichen on Bluff Mountain (The Nature Conservancy)

# elk knob state park

**Watauga County • 2,841 acres**

## Features

Elk Knob's heavily forested summit dominates the skyline of the region. A dense northern hardwood forest covers the mountain's steep slopes. The absence of stumps and old roadbeds suggest that portions of this forest may never have been logged. Rich forests dominate north-facing coves along larger streams on the mountain's lower slopes. Elk Knob is an important headwaters area for the New River, one of the oldest rivers in the world, and one of the very few rivers that flows south to north. The top of the 5,520-foot peak features great views of the surrounding landscape, including Mount Rogers, the highest point in Virginia.

The park boasts one of the greatest concentrations of rare plants in the southern Appalachians, including trailing wolfsbane, meehania, Roan rattlesnakeroot, and Gray's lily. The hardwood forest is dominated by northern red oak, yellow birch, and sugar maple.

Black bears inhabit this large block of unfragmented forest, as well as rare boreal creatures like the northern saw-whet owl and the globally endangered Carolina northern flying squirrel. Birders will enjoy Elk Knob's avian life: broad-winged hawks and ravens can be seen soaring overhead, and you are likely to hear ruffed grouse drumming during the breeding season. The many species of neotropical migratory songbirds that nest here include chestnut-sided warbler, black-throated blue warbler, ovenbird, scarlet tanager, and Canada warbler.

## Conservation Highlights

The 2002 purchase of Elk Knob enabled The Nature Conservancy to protect a significant part of the New River Headwaters. This area is particularly vulnerable to development pressures, since much of the land in the region is privately owned. In 2006, the Conservancy transferred ownership of the Elk Knob property to the N.C. Division of Parks and Recreation.

## Trip Planner

Elk Knob is one of the newest state parks, so facilities are limited and some trails are under development. Check with the park office, or consult the N.C. Division of Parks and Recreation web site, for the latest information.

At press time, hikers can reach the summit via an old road, which is a fairly rugged hike through rocks. Hikers should prepare for a strenuous trek and wear sturdy footwear. The top provides an inspiring three-state view that includes The Peak, Three Top and Bluff Mountains, Mount Mitchell, Grandfather Mountain, Mount Rogers (Virginia), and the Iron Mountains (Virginia and Tennessee).

Park officials conduct volunteer work days to help build a new, nicer trail to the summit. If you are interested in volunteering, contact the park office.

Elk Knob (Alan Cresswell)

## Ownership/Access

5564 Meat Camp Road
Todd, NC 28684
(828) 297-7261
elk.knob@ncmail.net
www.ncparks.gov

# paddy mountain preserve

**Ashe County • 262 acres**

## Features

The forested summit of Paddy Mountain towers over a bucolic landscape of pastures and Christmas tree farms. Part of the amphibolite mountains, which include Bluff and Three Top Mountains, Paddy has always been a fixture in the landscape, but its relative inaccessibility and lack of roads has kept it hidden.

From the lower slopes to its 4,331-foot summit, diverse habitats characterize Paddy's different elevations. Rich cove forests carpet the lowest slopes, particularly on the east side of the mountain. A variety of trees, including sugar maple, white ash, red oak, and shagbark hickory, provide a damp shady habitat for plants such as wild ginger, black cohosh, Solomon's seal, and maidenhair fern. Common mountain plants such as rhododendron, mountain laurel, and galax grow in chestnut oak forests on the northern slopes. Old-growth oak-hickory forests offer feeding and nesting grounds for neotropical song birds such as Canada warbler and rose-breasted grosbeak.

At higher elevations, there are exposed ridgetops. Here, the high-elevation rocky summits—expanses of irregular rock with scattered stunted trees and thin soil—offer a different habitat. Amphibolite rock weathers to a rich soil with a high pH that provides fertile ground for unique plant species, such as the world's largest population of the federally threatened Heller's blazing star, rare golden tundra moss, the federally endangered mountain bluet, and Michaux's saxifrage.

Paddy Mountain is just two air miles east of the Conservancy's Bluff Mountain Preserve and the state-owned Three Top Mountain Game Land. The proximity of these natural areas provides a much-needed corridor for animal species that need large areas of forest, including migratory birds and wide-ranging mammals such as black bear and bobcat.

## Conservation Highlights

In 2000, The Nature Conservancy purchased 228 acres of Paddy Mountain from the Rash family, who are longtime Ashe County residents. In 2002, the Conservancy transferred the property to the N.C. Plant Conservation Program.

## Trip Planner

This area contains rare, sensitive plants and can only be accessed by permit. For information on obtaining a permit contact the Plant Protection Section.

## Ownership/Access

N.C. Department of Agriculture
Plant Protection Section
P.O. 27647
Raleigh, NC 27611
(919) 733-3610
www.ncagr.gov/plantindustry/plant/plantconserve/mission.htm

Paddy Mountain (The Nature Conservancy)

# three top mountain game land

**Watauga County • 2,308 acres**

## Features

Three Top Mountain is named for the three rock outcrops that form the spine of the mountain's ridge. This area offers rugged hiking, cliffs, waterfalls, and great views. Elevations range from 3,000 to 4,800 feet above sea level. Three Top is part of the amphibolite mountain group, an unusual mountain chain containing a calcium-rich rock rare in the southern Blue Ridge. This group includes Mount Jefferson and Bluff Mountain, one of the North Carolina Chapter's best known preserves.

The ecosystem supports large populations of spreading avens, mountain bluet, Carolina saxifrage, and Heller's blazing star. Three Top offers good birding in the spring with opportunities to see nesting songbirds such as veery, rose-breasted grosbeak, chestnut-sided and Canada warblers, scarlet tanager, and red-eyed and solitary vireos.

## Conservation Highlights

In 1989 Chester Middlesworth offered to donate his 20 percent interest in a 1,100-acre parcel at Three Top. His generosity, combined with the willingness of the other four landowners to help the Conservancy, ensured the protection of the first portion of this project. Later, The Nature Conservancy purchased additional land from failed mountain developments.

## Trip Planner

This area has multiple uses, including hunting. Downloadable maps of the game land and hunting schedules are available on the Wildlife Resources Commission web site.

From West Jefferson drive north on NC 194/88. At Warrensville continue on NC 88 (over the New River Bridge), turn onto Peak Road (toward Creston), and then left on Three Top Road (also called Eller Road) and enter the Three Top Subdivision. Parking access is available on Three Top Road, on Hidden Valley Road, and on Edwards Road.

## Ownership/Access

N.C. Wildlife Resources Commission
1 (800) 662-7137
www.ncwildlife.org

Jonasee Rock (The Nature Conservancy)

# stone mountain state park

**Allegheny & Wilkes Counties**
**14,100 acres**

## Features

Located at the base of the Blue Ridge Escarpment, Stone Mountain is a granite dome that rises 600 feet above its base and is estimated to be 300 million years old. A type of granite dome known as a pluton, Stone Mountain became exposed as wind and water eroded the overlying soil layers over time. The bare monadnock emerges from dense hardwood forests—only stunted vegetation can grow on top of this bare mountain.

Stone Mountain was designated a National Natural Landmark in 1975. It lies in a beautiful area, bordered by the Blue Ridge Parkway to the north and by the Thurman Chatham Game Land to the west.

Wolf Rock and Cedar Rock, also located in the park, support diverse outcrop plant communities with many uncommon moss species, such as Keever's bristlemoss. Cove hardwood forests cover the lower slopes, while pine and oak forests dominate the rugged ridges. Hemlock, beech, and tulip poplar are some of the common trees in the park.

## Conservation Highlights

From 1975 to 1985, The Nature Conservancy protected 5,509 acres in the area, which were subsequently transferred to the N.C. Division of Parks and Recreation. Stone Mountain State Park is one of the largest parks in the state system.

## Trip Planner

Climbing is permitted in designated areas on the cliffs of Stone Mountain. Because of the dangers of rock climbing and rappelling, climbing is not recommended for beginners unless they are accompanied by an experienced climber. All climbers must register with the park by completing a climbing permit, which is available at the climbers' area at the base of the mountain.

The park includes more than 16 miles of hiking trails ranging from flat, easy paths to more strenuous climbs. Anglers will relish the park's 20 miles of designated trout waters, which are inhabited by rainbow, brown, and brook trout.

From the south, take US 21 (which intersects with I-77 west of Elkin), turn west onto Traphill Road (SR 1002), and go about four miles to Traphill and the John P. Frank Parkway. Continue 2.5 miles to the park entrance. From the west, take NC 18 north, turn right on Traphill Road, and follow it to the John P. Frank Parkway.

## Ownership/Access

N.C. Division of Parks and Recreation
3042 Frank Parkway
Roaring Gap, NC 28668
(336) 957-8185
stone.mountain@ncmail.net
www.ncparks/gov

Stone Mountain rock summit (Alan Cresswell)

# rendezvous mountain educational state forest

**Wilkes County • 3,040 acres**

## Features

The North Carolina Division of Forest Resources describes its educational forests as "living outdoor classrooms." Visitors to Rendezvous Mountain learn about the forest, its inhabitants, and its uses. One of the key features of Rendezvous Mountain is the half-mile "talking trees" trail. Each tree has a recorded message, which includes information about the species and its place in the ecosystem. Another trail is devoted to logging in western North Carolina. Both trails are designed with children in mind, so they're very easy strolls.

Rendezvous Mountain Educational State Forest is located in the transition area between the Piedmont and the Blue Ridge Mountains and contains plant communities characteristic of both regions. The 2,500-foot summit is located on the edge of Judd Mountain, a larger ridge sandwiched between two tributaries of the Yadkin River—the Reddies River and Lewis Fork Creek. Dense tangles of rhododendron cover the steep slopes and stream banks, while mountain laurel grows on the ridge tops.

The educational state forest lies on the eastern part of the mountain. It contains the mountain's most noteworthy natural feature—a remnant old-growth chestnut oak forest. Steep terrain prohibited logging in the area. As a result, trees 300 to 400 years old, measuring up to 30 inches in diameter, are found in the forest.

Shallow coves scattered through the forest contain rocky outcrops and seepage areas. Acidic cove forests cover most of these areas and the lower slopes of the mountain, and some rich cove forest is found here as well. Old chestnut stumps and logs throughout the mountain remind visitors of this once-abundant tree.

Black bear, white-tail deer, wild turkey, ruffed grouse, and migratory songbirds also call the forest home. Diverse plant life includes walking fern and spring-blooming wildflowers such as trilliums, Jack-in-the-pulpit, bloodroot, and pink lady slipper.

## Conservation Highlights

Judge T. B. Finley donated Rendezvous Mountain to the State of North Carolina in the 1920s. In 2001, The Nature Conservancy purchased 627 acres of hardwoods forest and transferred the property to the N.C. Division of Forest Resources.

## Trip Planner

The state forest is open from the third Wednesday in March to the day after Thanksgiving.

This is a great place for a school trip. Rangers are available to conduct field trips. Teachers can select from a series of half-hour programs that cover various aspects of the forest environment such as wildlife, soil,

Pink lady slipper (Bill Lea)

water, or forest management. Teachers wishing to bring large numbers of children should contact the forest office as early as possible to make reservations.

The forest contains a picnic area, restrooms and educational exhibits.

## Ownership/Access

N.C. Division of Forest Resources
Rendezvous Mountain Educational State Forest
1956 Rendezvous Mountain Road
Purlear, NC 28651
(336) 667-5072
rendezvousmountainESF.DFR@ncmail.net
www.dfr.state.nc.us

# greater roan highlands

K NOWN FOR ITS RHODODENDRON DISPLAYS IN LATE SPRING AND EARLY SUMMER, THIS AREA CONTAINS 10 MILES OF THE APPALACHIAN TRAIL THAT HIGHLIGHT THE SPRUCE-FIR FORESTS OF ROAN HIGH KNOB (6,286 FEET) AND THE HEATH AND GRASSY BALD ON ROUND BALD (5,826 FEET). The heavy snow and "rime" ice that occur from December through April give the area an equally stunning appearance in winter, although access can be hazardous. The highlands also contain northern hardwood forest downslope from the spruce-fir forests and the balds.

## Features

Many small mammals and raptors frequent the area, with the New England cottontail, northern flying squirrel, and northern saw-whet owl near the southern extent of their ranges. Birding opportunities include some rare and local nesting species such as hermit thrush and alder flycatcher. Dozens of rare plants are found in the Roan Mountain Highlands, including federally listed species such as spreading avens, Blue Ridge goldenrod, and mountain bluet. Other notable rarities found in the area include Gray's lily, bent avens, and Schweinitz's ragwort.

## Conservation Highlights

In the late 1970s, The Nature Conservancy helped protect portions of this unique area on behalf of the U.S. Forest Service. These purchases extended Pisgah Forest lands around Roan Mountain and are near Tennessee's Roan Mountain State Park. The Nature Conservancy and the Southern Appalachian Highlands Conservancy jointly manage nearby Big Yellow Mountain, which is also featured in this guide.

## Trip Planner

From the junction of NC 226 and NC 261 in Bakersville, take NC 261 north almost 13 miles to Carver's Gap on the North Carolina/Tennessee line. Follow SR 1348, a two-mile spur road from Carver's Gap, to the Roan summit parking and trails. There is a small fee per vehicle for access to the top of the mountain. A trailhead for the Appalachian Trail at Carver's Gap goes to Round Bald.

from left: (John Warner) Bald coated in ice (Kim Hadley)

# big yellow mountain preserve

**Avery County • 426 acres**

## Features

At 5,540 feet, Big Yellow's open, grassy peak offers a vantage point from which you can look out over range after range of the Blue Ridge Mountains. Part of the Roan Highlands, Big Yellow is a grassy bald, an unusual community type that resembles a high-elevation pasture and is found between 5,200 and 5,800 feet on dome-shaped summits and ridges. Possibly remnants from the last ice age, these "sky islands" have a principally northern climate in a southern location and harbor unique species requiring cool temperatures and lots of sunlight. The origin of the balds is unclear, but they were probably formed by a variety of factors, such as climate, grazing, and human-ignited fires. We do know that elk and bison roamed in the area prior to European settlement and probably grazed on the balds, maintaining their open quality. Cattle still graze on the bald to maintain the area.

Three-toothed cinquefoil and mountain oat grass are the predominant vegetation on Big Yellow. An abundance of wildflowers, including Gray's lily, Turk's cap lily, and fringed phacelia, are found on the bald and in the surrounding forests from the spring to the fall. The largest known southeastern population of Schweinitz's groundsel is found in slightly sheltered, steep, hummocky areas on the preserve. This plant is a northern disjunct species found on a few grassy balds in North Carolina.

Several species of shrews, moles, and weasels have been seen at Big Yellow, along with larger mammals such as black bear and bobcat. Monarch butterflies often congregate in large numbers here during their fall migration in September and October. The bald is also a fine vantage point for observing migrating raptors in the fall, including an occasional golden eagle.

## Conservation Highlights

The Nature Conservancy acquired this tract in 1975 from the Avery family, who had owned it since 1785. The Conservancy has since transferred some land to the U.S. Forest Service. The Nature Conservancy and the Southern Appalachian Highlands Conservancy jointly manage 395 acres. Because long-term, low-level grazing is needed to preserve this natural community, The Nature Conservancy and the Southern Appalachians Highlands Conservancy continue to graze cattle on the bald.

## Trip Planner

Both The Nature Conservancy and Southern Appalachian Highlands Conservancy periodically offer field trips to the preserve. Call North Carolina Mountains Office at (828) 350-1431 or contact the Southern Appalachian Highlands Conservancy, www.appalachian.org, 34 Wall Street, Suite 802, Asheville, NC 28801-2710, (828) 253-0095.

Cows grazing on Big Yellow Mountain (John Warner)

## Ownership/Access

The Nature Conservancy
P.O. Box 17519
Asheville, NC 28816
(828) 350-1431
www.nature.org/northcarolina

# grandfather mountain

## Features

Naturalists have long recognized Grandfather's special beauty. When John Muir visited the site in the 1890s he said the mountain was "the face of all heaven come to earth." A century after Muir's visit, the United Nations recognized Grandfather Mountain as an International Biosphere Reserve. The North Carolina Natural Heritage Program has done important work at the site, documenting its ecological significance. Thanks to that work, Grandfather Mountain has been a Registered Natural Heritage Area since 1979.

Famous for its rocky summits, cliffs, and great views of the Blue Ridge Mountains and Piedmont, Grandfather Mountain is one of North Carolina's most biologically diverse mountains. Rock outcrops, spruce-fir forests, heath balds, and hardwood forests provide habitat for over 60 rare plant and animal species, including the Carolina northern flying squirrel, Weller's salamander, and four endangered plants: spreading avens, Heller's blazing star, mountain bluet, and Blue Ridge goldenrod. Grandfather is near the southern end of the range of species such as the northern saw-whet owl, hermit thrush, and New England cottontail.

One of the more unique species that the Conservancy keeps an eye on at Grandfather is the spruce-fir moss spider, a tiny tarantula that grows no larger than the head of a thumbtack. It lives only above 5,000 feet, in moss mats under spruce and Fraser fir trees. Grandfather Mountain, Roan Mountain, and Great Smoky Mountains National Park harbor the only known populations of this spider. The species has become increasingly rare as spruce-fir forests have declined because of a combination of air pollution and the balsam woolly adelgid, a nonnative insect that takes sap from the fir trees.

## Conservation Highlights

The late conservationist Hugh Morton inherited Grandfather Mountain in 1952, operating 600 acres as a tourist attraction that included the famous mile-high swinging bridge, a nature museum, and various wildlife habitats. Morton had a strong conservation ethic, and he worked to ensure that much of the area remained undeveloped; he took care to instill in visitors a knowledge of the importance of mountain ecosystems, 16 of which are represented at Grandfather. Morton died in 2006.

In September 2008, the Morton family announced that it was selling the 2,601 acres of undeveloped land to the N.C. Division of Parks and Recreation, making Grandfather Mountain North Carolina's 34th state park. The deal also included a conservation easement on the 600-acre tourist attraction, which would be managed as a nonprofit entity

Grandfather Mountain (Bill Lea)

by Morton's heirs. The $12 million dollar purchase was made possible by the Natural Heritage Trust Fund and the Parks and Recreation Trust Fund.

This deal was the culmination of a preservation partnership that stretches back almost two decades. Without this partnership involving the Morton family, The Nature Conservancy, The Conservation Fund, and state government, Grandfather Mountain State Park would not have come into existence.

The Nature Conservancy first partnered with the Morton family in 1990, when Hugh Morton donated 146 acres of conservation easements to the Conservancy. Over the years, the Conservancy's efforts on Grandfather grew to the protection of 1,800 acres through conservation easements and another thousand acres bought outright by the Conservancy. The Conservancy has also monitored another thousand acres of easements, which were purchased by the Clean Water Management Trust Fund.

## Trip Planner

The entrance to Grandfather Mountain is on the north side of US 221 between the Blue Ridge Parkway and the town of Linville. The trails on Grandfather offer a variety of hiking options, from easy walks through beautiful hardwood forests to rugged hikes to the highest point on the mountain, 5,964-foot Calloway Peak. If you visit Grandfather from mid-April through mid-July, you will be treated to many showy wildflowers. The mountain is also a good place for birding, offering migratory birds in the spring such as Canada and Blackburnian warblers,

rose-breasted grosbeak, and scarlet tanager, and migrating broad-winged hawks in the fall.

For information on the tourist attractions operated by the Morton heirs, go to their web site, www.grandfather.com. Plans for North Carolina's newest park are incomplete at press time. Any additional facilities will be identified through a public master park planning process. In the meantime, hikers wanting to use the park's trails should contact Grandfather Mountain, Inc.

The Nature Conservancy also conducts guided hikes to its Grandfather Mountain Preserve; information on those hikes can be obtained through the North Carolina Mountains Office.

### Ownership and Access

Grandfather Mountain State Park (under development)
N.C. Division of Parks and Recreation
1615 MSC
Raleigh N.C. 27699-1615
(919) 733-4181

Grandfather Mountain Private Attraction
Grandfather Mountain, Inc.
P.O. Box 129
Linville, NC 28646
(800) 468-7325 • (828) 733-2013

Grandfather Mountain Preserve and Conservation Easements
The Nature Conservancy
P.O. Box 17519
Asheville, NC 28816
(828) 350-1431
www.nature.org/northcarolina

(John Warner)

# celo knob

## Features

Located in the Black Mountains area of Pisgah National Forest, just north of Mount Mitchell State Park, Celo (SEE-Low) Knob is a great example of a high-elevation mountain forest. Elevations vary from 3,200 feet to the 6,327-foot Celo Knob, a local landmark. Because of its rugged topography, much of Celo Knob is inaccessible. This area contains old-growth boreal forest, northern hardwood and cove hardwood forest, dry ridges and heath balds, and one of the most extensive examples of red spruce/fraser fir forest in the southern Appalachians. If you visit Celo Knob, you will notice that some of the spruce-fir forest has been damaged by the deadly duo of air pollution and the balsam woolly adelgid, an exotic invasive pest.

This range is home to many plant species that are endangered or rare in the state, including mountain paper birch, fir clubmoss, Carolina saxifrage, Core's starwort, red raspberry, and roseroot. Some of the uncommon fauna that inhabit the area are the Carolina northern flying squirrel, northern saw-whet owl, brown creeper, common raven, golden-crowned kinglet, red-breasted nuthatch, and New England cottontail. Several rugged trails run through the area. While hiking you may see remnants of mica mines in various stages of recovery.

## Conservation Highlights

The Nature Conservancy purchased a 2,408-acre tract from the Briggs family in 1978 and subsequently transferred it to the U.S. Forest Service.

## Trip Planner

Be prepared for a strenuous climb. The Celo Knob hike is extremely tough. Experienced hikers say it is one of the more difficult treks on the East Coast.

Head south from Burnsville on Low Gap Road (SR 1109) about two miles. Forest Road (SR 5578) turns left at Bowlens Creek. This rough road leads up to an approximately five-mile trail to Celo Knob. This trail continues by following the ridge top south to Horse Rock Ridge and Mount Mitchell, about 12 miles from the Bowlens Creek parking area.

## Ownership/Access

U.S. Forest Service
Appalachian Ranger District
P.O. Box 128
Burnsville, NC 28714
(828) 682-6146
www.cs.unca.edu/nfsnc

Mountain rhododendrons (Bill Lea)

# mount mitchell state park

**Yancey County • 1,855 acres**

## Features

At 6,684 feet above sea level, Mount Mitchell is the highest peak in the eastern United States and contains an extensive area of spruce-fir forest, one of the country's rarest ecosystems. Spruce-fir forest is abundant in a large region of northern North America, but south of New England the forest type is only found in a narrow band in the Appalachian Mountains. This natural community is characterized by evergreens, particularly red spruce and Fraser fir, and harbors many species that are closely related to species in the spruce-fir forests of New England.

In North Carolina, spruce-fir forest occurs at elevations above 5,500 feet, where cool temperatures and high moisture are prevalent conditions. The forests are remnants from the last ice age some 18,000 years ago and have become refuges for species that cannot tolerate warmer, drier conditions. This forest type is declining due to the negative effects of air pollution, climate disruption, and the balsam woolly adelgid, an exotic pest.

Many rare plants are found at the park, including the state's only population of mountain paper birch and one of only a few global populations of Cain's reedgrass. The federally listed endangered spreading avens also grows in the park.

Some of the uncommon animals that inhabit Mount Mitchell are the federally listed endangered northern flying squirrel, New England cottontail, bobcat, and many species of salamander. Some of the birds that breed here are more typical of northern conifer forests: red-breasted nuthatch, brown creeper, and golden-crowned kinglet. Visit the park in the fall to see migrating hawks and monarch butterflies.

## Conservation Highlights

The State of North Carolina established its first state park at Mount Mitchell in 1915 to protect the area's virgin Fraser fir from timbering. The North Carolina Chapter purchased 84 acres of additional land for Mount Mitchell State Park in 1997.

## Trip Planner

The park is located just off the Blue Ridge Parkway (north of Balsam Gap), 33 miles northeast of Asheville. Follow the parkway to milepost 355.4, turn north on NC 128, and go 2.4 miles to the park entrance.

### Ownership/Access

N.C. Division of Parks and Recreation
2388 State Highway 128, Burnsville, NC 28714
(828) 675-4611
mount.mitchell@ncmail.net
www.ncparks.gov

Mount Mitchell (USDA Natural Resources Conservation Service)

# plott balsams preserve

## Features

The Plott Balsams Range casts a long shadow over the rugged territory between Sylva and Waynesville. Ranging from 2,100 feet in elevation near Sylva to more than 6,000 feet at Yellow Face and Waterrock Knob on the Blue Ridge Parkway, the mountain range rises more than 4,000 feet in elevation in less than eight miles. Named for the German immigrants who settled the area in 1750, the Plott Balsams intersect the Great Balsam Range at Waterrock Knob.

More than 90 percent of the preserve is forest, interrupted by the occasional rock outcrop or boulder. Due to the change in elevation, the reserve includes northern hardwood forest, acidic cove forest, and rich cove forest. The higher reaches of the range contain significant spruce-fir forest, as well as old-growth forest in the most inaccessible areas.

Black bear, common raven, ruffed grouse, and wild turkey live on the preserve. The spruce-fir forest provides a refuge for rare boreal species such as the federally endangered Carolina northern flying squirrel and the northern saw-whet owl, a species of special concern in North Carolina. Rare plant species such as the federally listed rock gnome lichen and pink-shell azalea (almost entirely limited to North Carolina) grow on high-elevation rocky summits in the mountain range, while colorful wildflowers like showy orchis grow in the hardwood forests.

## Conservation Highlights

In 1997, The Nature Conservancy purchased the 1,595-acre Krauss/Stansbury tract. The property borders two miles of the Blue Ridge Parkway.

## Trip Plannor

If you aren't prepared for a strenuous hike, you can see the Plott Balsams from several overlooks on the Blue Ridge Parkway from mileposts 451 to 465.

The strenuous hike to the top of Waterrock Knob takes off at mile 451.2. The parking area at the trailhead has restrooms and a small visitor center. The 1.2 mile roundtrip trail is paved for the first quarter mile and then turns into a rugged rocky trail. Upon reaching the summit, hardy hikers are rewarded with panoramic views of several mountain ranges including the Smokies, Great Balsams, Pisgah Ridge, and Blacks.

You can also hike from Waterrock Knob to Pinnacle Park in Sylva. This hike will take you through Plott Balsams Preserve. The trail begins across from the driveway to Waterrock Knob Visitor Center on the Blue Ridge Parkway. It follows the ridgeline, crossing the Plott Balsams Preserve to Black Rock, which is at the edge of Pinnacle Park in Sylva. The trail is moderately strenuous, requiring some scrambling and climbing. The roundtrip trek will take approximately four and a half hours. At press time, work is continuing on a spur trail that would take hikers through the park and to the Pinnacle.

Showy orchis (Bill Lea)

## Ownership/Access

The Nature Conservancy
P.O. Box 17519
Asheville, NC 28816
(828) 350-1431
www.nature.org/northcarolina

# richland balsam mountain preserve

**Jackson County • 262 acres**

## Features

Richland Balsam Mountain Preserve is located on the south slope of the 6,400-foot Richland Balsam Mountain, the highest point in the Great Balsam Range and the highest point along the Blue Ridge Parkway. One side of the nature preserve borders the parkway and the other side borders Nantahala National Forest. Spruce-fir forests historically blanketed the Balsam range, but since the mid-1970s, Fraser fir forests have declined precipitously. Spruce-fir forest is considered one of the rarest and most threatened ecosystems in North America.

Until the late 1970s, the top of Richland Balsam was cloaked in a thick cover of Fraser firs. However, the forest has suffered greatly from the combined effects of the balsam woolly adelgid and air pollution. The adelgid—a native of Europe—was introduced into America around 1900, probably through infested nursery stock. European trees are not susceptible to the adelgid, but American trees sicken and die as the adelgid infests and feeds on them. The adelgid's work can be seen on the summit, which now consists of dead trees above dense stands of shrubs and seedling firs.

Northern hardwood forests blanket the lower slopes, and an orchard-like high elevation red oak forest is found on the southern slope. Grassy bald-like openings dot the southwestern slope below the peak. The preserve also contains high-elevation wetlands.

Birders will enjoy keeping an eye out for uncommon boreal species such as the black-capped chickadee and northern saw-whet owl, which nest on the preserve. Other interesting birds that have been documented at the preserve include black-billed cuckoo, red crossbill, and pine siskin.

The federally endangered Carolina northern flying squirrel, a diminutive arboreal acrobat, inhabits the preserve, as well as an endemic ground beetle and the rare Mary Alice's small-headed fly.

Rare plants such as large-leaved grass-of-Parnassus, Appalachian clubmoss, and pinkshell azalea grow on the preserve.

## Conservation Highlights

In 1996, Mr. Russell Beutell generously donated all 262 acres of the Richland Balsam Mountain Preserve to The Nature Conservancy.

## Trip Planner

Richland Balsam Overlook at mile 431.4 on the Blue Ridge Parkway is the highest point on the parkway. It is also the trailhead for the National Park Service 1.5 mile self-guided loop trail that climbs to the summit of Richland Balsam Mountain. In summer and leaf season, the overlook can get very crowded, but most people don't choose to hike. The trail is moderate to strenuous, gaining 500 feet in altitude. On a clear day, hikers can see Mount Mitchell and the Black Mountains.

Morel mushroom (Ida Phillips)

## Ownership/Access

The Nature Conservancy
P.O. Box 17519
Asheville, NC 28816
(828) 350-1431
www.nature.org/northcarolina

# needmore game land

## Features

Needmore is the collective name for multiple land parcels totaling over 4,400 acres on a 27-mile stretch of the Little Tennessee River between Franklin, North Carolina, and Fontana Lake. The largest parcel, 4,000 contiguous acres, consists of 3,400 acres in Swain County and 600 acres in Macon County. Twelve noncontiguous parcels in Macon County account for the remaining 400 or so acres.

In the millions of years since the glaciers retreated, individual watersheds like the Little Tennessee, isolated and boasting benign environmental conditions, provided a perfect setting for the evolution of unique species of plants, invertebrates, salamanders, crayfish, freshwater mussels, and fishes. These species were likely found throughout the Southern Appalachians at one time, but survive in the Little Tennessee because the river has been minimally affected by dams, development, and pollution that have radically altered the biology of nearly all rivers in the Southeast.

Sandwiched between the Nantahala and the Cowee mountain ranges, this area until recently had not seen the same development pressures that have changed the landscape in many other places near the Great Smoky Mountains National Park. In the 1930s, the Needmore tract was created out of smaller landholdings when utilities bought property to build a reservoir to generate hydropower.

Those plans never became economically feasible, and much of the property remained in its wild state.

The Needmore land contains more than 27 miles of riparian frontage on the Little Tennessee River and includes more than 45 miles of the 160 tributaries that feed it. There are 72 isolated wetlands here, and more than 80 percent of the property is within 300 feet of the Little Tennessee River and its tributaries. Lack of development has kept the river's water clean and allowed its tributaries to remain important nurseries for a number of rare aquatic species. Forty-seven native fish species are found in the game land, as well as four federally listed species, including the spotfin chub and the Appalachian elktoe mussel, and 12 state-listed species, including the sicklefin redhorse (a fish) and hellbender salamander.

While aquatic and amphibian species get the most attention on Needmore, the game land also provides important habitat for a large number of other plants and animals. Due to its largely forested condition and its geographic location along a north-south migratory route through the Southern Appalachians, it is a seasonal home to a number of rare warbler species, including the cerulean.

Insects, such as the tawny crescent butterfly, and a wide variety of bats can be found on the property, which rises in elevation from 1,640 to 2,160 feet above sea level. The terrain varies from near level floodplains to steep cliffs. There are also low, rolling hills, drainages, coves, bluffs, and rock outcrops that provide

Little Tennessee River (The Nature Conservancy)

habitat for game, including black bear, grouse, and turkey. Botanists have identified a number of rare plants on the property including Huger's carrionflower, Virginia spirea, and southern nodding trillium.

## Conservation Highlights

As part of its Forever Wild campaign in 2004, The Nature Conservancy purchased the Needmore tracts from Crescent Resources, LLC, and transferred them to the N.C. Wildlife Resources Commission. The transaction concluded more than three years of negotiations. The Conservancy raised $2 million in private funds, which were combined with public monies from the Clean Water Management Trust Fund, the Ecosystem Enhancement Program, the Natural Heritage Trust Fund, and the U.S. Fish and Wildlife Service to meet the $19 million price tag on the property.

## Trip Planner

A good way to see Needmore is by paddling on the Little Tennessee River. There are unmaintained and unmarked hiking trails in the game land. If you hike in the game land, please bring detailed topo maps and a compass. This area has multiple uses, including hunting. Downloadable maps of the game land, hunting schedules, and paddling access ways are available on the Wildlife Resources Commission web site.

## Ownership/Access

N.C. Wildlife Resources Commission
1 (800) 662-7137
www.ncwildlife.org

# nantahala national forest

THE NATURE CONSERVANCY PLAYED A MAJOR ROLE IN PROTECTING LANDS THAT ARE NOW PART OF THE 531,338-ACRE NANTAHALA NATIONAL FOREST IN EXTREME SOUTHWEST NORTH CAROLINA. The largest of North Carolina's four national forests, Nantahala offers a wide range of recreational opportunities, including some of the toughest hikes in the Southeast.

"Nantahala" is a Cherokee word that means "land of the noonday sun." That's a fitting name: in some of the steep forest gorges, the sun only reaches the valley floor in the middle of the day. The U.S. Forest Service describes this area as a "land of granite walls and waterfalls."

from left: Panthertown Schoolhouse Falls (Hart Matthews) Bonas Defeat Gorge (David Ray)

# bonas defeat gorge/balsam area

## Features

Some of the area's most challenging hikes are found at Bonas Defeat and the Balsam Area (also known as the Roy Taylor Forest), which is managed as part of the Nantahala National Forest. This property borders the south side of the Blue Ridge Parkway for nine miles just west of NC 215 near Tuckasegee. According to local legend, Bonas was a hunting dog who met his fate while chasing a deer over a 400-foot cliff on this property in the 19th century.

The Balsam Area contains outstanding natural features including high peaks, 70 miles of trout streams, valley gorges, eight waterfalls, and outstanding views. As elevations in this tract vary from 2,500 feet to 5,500 feet, two distinct ecosystems occur here: the Appalachian oak forest and the southern Appalachian spruce-fir forest at the highest elevations.

One of the most rugged parts of the Blue Ridge region, this area contains the headwaters of four creeks that drain into the Tuckasegee River, along with four peaks over 5,000 feet. Many potholes, cascades, and large boulders distinguish the streambeds in Bonas Defeat's rocky gorge. Cove and hemlock forests dominate the slopes of the gorge. Several northern species, such as the northern saw-whet owl, northern flying squirrel, and New England cottontail reach the southern end of their range here.

## Conservation Highlights

Over half of this land was owned by the Mead Corporation and then sold to a development company for summer homes. The downturn in the economy in the late 1970s made this opportunity less attractive, leading to its sale for conservation. The Nature Conservancy purchased this area in 1981 on behalf of the U.S. Forest Service for $13.4 million as an addition to Nantahala National Forest.

## Trip Planner

The trails in this area are primitive and are close to private property, so be sure to bring your topo maps. This is rugged territory and only experienced, conditioned, and well-equipped hikers should take the trek to Bonas Defeat. Check with the Ranger District Office to get up-to-date information about trail conditions. During periods of heavy rain or when water is released in the gorge, flash flooding occurs, so do not attempt this hike if it is raining.

The Balsam Area can be viewed from the Blue Ridge Parkway. A short asphalt walkway leads to an observation deck at mile 433.8. A short unmarked trail around Tanasee Bald and Herrin Knob starts at the Blue Ridge Parkway picnic area at mile 423.5.

## Ownership/Access

Nantahala National Forest
Nantahala Ranger District
90 Sloan Road
Franklin, NC 28734
(828) 524-6441
www.cs.unca.edu/nfsnc

Bonas Defeat Gorge (David Ray)

# panthertown valley

**Jackson, Macon, & Transylvania Counties • 6,295 acres**

## Features

Panthertown Valley, which is managed as part of Nantahala National Forest, is a treat for hikers, as it contains a curious mixture of threatened and endangered species and natural communities. Panthertown is distinguished by its broad flat valley floor flanked by granite cliffs abruptly rising 200 to 300 feet. These granite domes with exposed rock are uncommon in the Southern Appalachians and offer spectacular open vistas. The unusually flat valley is home to at least 11 different natural communities, including the rare Southern Appalachian bog and the swamp forest-bog community. These communities harbor numerous rare plants, such as Cuthbert's turtlehead, Canada burnet, marsh bellflower, climbing fern, and spinulose wood fern.

The headwaters of the East Fork of the Tuckasegee River and 20 miles of native brook trout streams, including Panthertown, Greenland, and Flat Creeks, are located in Panthertown Valley.

## Conservation Highlights

In 1989 the North Carolina Chapter purchased this tract from Duke Power Company for $8 million as an addition to Nantahala National Forest. Panthertown Valley is located in a very popular vacation home and resort area in the North Carolina mountains, so it was unusual to find such a large piece of land under single ownership.

## Trip Planner

Hiking on the old logging roads of Panthertown is a good way to familiarize yourself with this large scenic valley. A network of hiking trails will lead you to waterfalls and spectacular overlooks of the valley, its cliff faces, and bogs. The waterfalls have a wet microclimate supporting the highest concentration of rare plants in the valley.

Most of the trails in Pantertown Valley are unmarked, so hikers should bring a good trail map or topo map of the area. Slickrock Expeditions sells a trail map of Panthertown Valley called *A Guide's Guide to Panthertown Valley*. For ordering information, visit the Slickrock Expeditions web site, www.slickrockexpeditions.com.

Please be aware that there are many sensitive areas in Panthertown Valley. Hikers can lessen their impact by staying on designated trails. The rare ferns, mosses, and liverworts near the waterfalls are easily scraped off the rocks when visitors walk behind the falls. For this reason, the U.S. Forest Service encourages visitors to view the falls from below.

Primitive overnight camping and catch-and-release fishing are allowed in Panthertown, so you can spend a full weekend in this wild area.

There are several entrances to Panthertown Valley, but the most accessible route is as follows: Approximately two miles east of Cashiers on US 64, turn left or north on Cedar Creek Road (SR 1120). Continue on Cedar

Cove hardwood forest (Bill Lea)

Creek Road 2.2 miles. Bear right (northeast) on Breedlove Road (SR 1121). Continue 3.4 miles on SR 1121 to a flat parking area at a gap where the National Forest boundary begins. The access road from the gap makes an excellent foot travel path. No motor vehicles are allowed beyond this point.

## Ownership/Access

Nantahala National Forest
Nantahala Ranger District
90 Sloan Road
Franklin, NC 28734
(828) 524-6441
www.cs.unca.edu/nfsnc

# standing indian mountain

## Features

Like many places in this region, the mountain gets its name from a Cherokee legend: A child was kidnapped by an evil monster. The tribe sent a warrior to wait on the mountain top, looking for the child's return. Other villagers prayed for the Great Spirit to kill the monster. The Great Spirit sent a storm, turning the warrior and the mountain top into stone. Today, the standing Indian continues to guard the area.

The mountain is located in a rugged backcountry area southwest of the town of Franklin and adjacent to the 23,472-acre Southern Nantahala National Wilderness Area, which is split between North Carolina and Georgia. The area is studded with peaks over 4,000 feet. At 5,499 feet, Standing Indian Mountain dominates the scene.

Standing Indian Mountain contains a mixture of many of the natural communities typically found in the Southern Appalachians. Portions of this heavily forested area contain relatively undisturbed habitats, including northern hardwood forest and a high-elevation red oak forest. Rocky outcrops, scrubby heath balds, and seepage areas are found on the highest, exposed ridgetops. Nine species of rare plants have been documented in the area, including the showy purple fringeless orchid, lichens, and liverworts. Ruffed grouse and black bear are among the many creatures that inhabit the region.

## Conservation Highlights

The Nature Conservancy helped purchase 1,492 acres of the mountain in the early 1960s and later transferred the property to the U.S. Forest Service. The wilderness area was designated in 1984.

## Trip Planner

From the junction of US 64 and US 441/23 west of Franklin, take US 64 west for nine miles. Turn left on Old US 64 (Wallace Gap Road) and follow the road 1.5 miles to Forest Road (FR) 67. Turn right and drive 1.5 miles to reach Standing Indian Campground. Or continue driving on FR 67 for a total of 2.1 miles to reach the backcountry information center. The road continues south for nine miles, and you can access trailheads along the road.

Seventy miles of hiking trails run through the area, including 20 miles of the Appalachian Trail. The hike to Standing Indian Mountain summit is a tough-going five miles.

Standing Indian Campground contains 84 campsites and is open April through November. In the summer, it is very busy and camping spaces are hard to come by. You can call the campground at (828) 369-0442 to reserve spaces; on most weekends, there is a two-day mandatory advance reservation.

## Ownership/Access

Nantahala National Forest
Nantahala Ranger District
90 Sloan Road
Franklin, NC 28734
(828) 524-6441
www.cs.unca.edu/nfsnc

Spring in the Nantahala (Bill Lea)

# blue ridge escarpment gorges

T HE STEEP PLUNGE OF THE BLUE RIDGE ESCARPMENT CREATES DEEP GORGES AND DRAMATIC WATERFALLS. Many of those waterfalls are on public property—some easily accessible by the public, some entailing more difficult hikes.

Geographically, the Jocassee Gorges comprise roughly 50,000 acres in North and South Carolina, where the escarpment of the Blue Ridge Mountains rises dramatically from the Piedmont to nearly 4,000 feet above sea level.

Five powerful rivers—the Whitewater, Thompson, Toxaway, Chattooga, and Horsepasture—wind through the area. The Chattooga and Horsepasture are both classified as National Wild and Scenic Rivers.

One of the wettest places in eastern North America, this wild area is shaped by the forces of water. On average, between 70 and 80 inches of rain fall here every year, although an annual amount of 100 inches is not uncommon. The escarpment has one of the greatest concentrations of waterfalls in the eastern United States and contains a great variety of natural habitats, such as oak forests, cove forests, granite domes, and scattered patches of old-growth forest in the most rugged areas.

Abundant wildlife inhabits the area, including black bear, bobcat, and wild turkey, North Carolina's largest known population of the rare green salamander, native trout, and several species of rare fish. Neotropical migratory songbirds such as the uncommon Swainson's warbler occur in large numbers in the Gorges. The escarpment harbors one of the highest concentrations of rare plants in North America, with over 60 rare species identified to date. As the climate in other areas has changed, the Blue Ridge Escarpment has been a long-term refuge for plants dependent on high humidity and a moderate climate. Many of the fern, moss, and liverwort species found in the Gorges are more commonly found in the wet tropics. Up to 90 percent of the world's populations of rare Oconee bells are found in the Gorges region; its nearest relatives are found in China and Japan.

from left: Eagle Rock (The Nature Conservancy) Trilliums and stream (Bill Lea)

# silver run preserve

**Jackson & Transylvania Counties**
**1,483 acres**

## Features

Silver Run Preserve is the largest Conservancy-owned preserve along the Southern Blue Ridge Escarpment.

A biological inventory of Silver Run Preserve has been completed, and scientists have found specimens or habitat for federally and globally imperiled plant species that have been identified nearby, including pinkshell azalea, Fraser's loosestrife, rock gnome lichen, and the small whorled pogonia. The property contains excellent examples of a number of natural communities such as rock outcrops, spray cliff, and seepage communities. It supports healthy populations of bear, deer, and turkey.

## Conservation Highlights

The preserve, surrounded on three sides by the Nantahala National Forest, is the headwaters of the Whitewater River and was donated to the Conservancy from the estate of Ernest Willis in December 2003.

## Trip Planner

This Nature Conservancy preserve is only accessible through the North Carolina Chapter's field trip program. Contact the North Carolina Mountains Office at (828) 350-1431 for details.

## Ownership/Access

The Nature Conservancy
P.O. Box 17519
Asheville, NC 28816
(828) 350-1431
www.nature.org/northcarolina

Silver Run (The Nature Conservancy)

Silver Run Falls (The Nature Conservancy)

# gorges state park

## Features

Transylvania County is appropriately called "Land of Waterfalls," for the 250 or so waterfalls found in the county. Many of the most beautiful of those falls are found in Gorges State Park. Parts of the park are quite rugged, with an elevation change of 2,000 feet in just four miles.

The park is home to 125 rare plant and animal species and has been designated an area of national ecological significance by the state's Natural Heritage Program. Two species of moss that are normally found in much more southerly areas are found in the park. The Carolina star-moss, with its dark green rosettes, thrives in waterfall spray; it is found only in the Southern Appalachians and the Dominican Republic. Pringle's aquatic moss is found on rocks under the waterfalls; it occurs only in the Southern Appalachians and Mexico. The fragile Gorge filmy-fern, Appalachian filmy-fern, and dwarf filmy-fern also live in the park; they get the name "filmy" because they are only a single cell thick. They can survive only in the constant humidity provided by waterfall spray. Other plant species include rhododendron and mountain laurel, which put on a colorful spring flower show.

Probably the most famous of the park's flowering plants is the Oconee bells, a federally endangered species. Oconee bells are characterized by white flowers on single stalks above evergreen leaves. They bloom in March and April.

The park is also home to black bear, fox, wild turkey, deer, and the occasional wild boar. Wild boar is an introduced species and is one of the threats listed in the Conservancy's Conservation Action Plan for the Southern Blue Ridge Escarpment landscape area. The Jocassee Gorges house the state's largest population of rare green salamander, which can be found in rock crevices. They are perfectly adapted to live in the narrow crevices because they have a generally flat head and body.

## Conservation Highlights

Many conservation organizations and agencies, including The Nature Conservancy, the N.C. Division of Parks and Recreation, N.C. Wildlife Resources Commission, U.S. Forest Service, Sierra Club, and the Wildlife Federation worked to acquire and protect the Gorges. The State of North Carolina appropriated $5 million for the property and, in 1999, purchased 9,641 acres from Duke Energy. The Division of Parks and Recreation manages 6,725 acres in a state park. The remaining 2,916 acres was added to the N.C. Wildlife Resources Commission's Toxaway Game Land.

## Trip Planner

Gorges is a relatively new addition to the state park system, so much of the park is still in the interim or planning stages. The interim park office is housed with the Sapphire Post Office at the intersection of NC 281 and US 264.

From Brevard take US 64 west, traveling

toward Sapphire. Take a left onto Frozen Creek Road; the east park entrance is three miles down the road on the right. To reach the west entrance turn south on NC 281 in Sapphire; the Grassy Ridge entrance, is 0.7 mile on the left.

Strong hikers will enjoy the park's back-country treks, where steep trails offer a chance to see waterfalls. Before undertaking a back-country visit, check in at the park office—some of the area is extremely rugged and could be dangerous for people who aren't in good physical shape or properly outfitted. A popular hike is the Foothills trail, which winds along Lake Jocassee. Look for the trailhead access on Frozen Creek Road near the town of Rosman. There are six primitive camp sites located 5.5 miles down the trail. Another six primitive camp sites can be reached by a 2.7 mile hike from the Grassy Ridge Access point. The Grassy Ridge Access point is also the trailhead for the waterfall overlook trail, which begins near the parking lot and is marked with blue circles.

The Wildlife Resources Toxaway Game Land is accessible by foot from Whitewater Falls Road (SR 1149), traveling south to South Carolina. The only road access to the game land is through the park. If you wish to access the game land by road, then you need to get permission and gate keys from the state park several days in advance. Remember this area has multiple uses, including hunting. Downloadable maps of the game land and hunting schedules are available on the Wildlife Resources Commission web site, www.ncwildlife.org.

At press time, the N.C. Division of Parks

Gorges State Park (Charlie Peek)

and Recreation had signed a contract that will allow park visitors to make advance registration for campsites, shelters, and other facilities via a toll-free number and online. The system should be functional by summer 2009 and information will be posted on the park web site, www.ncparks.gov.

## Ownership/Access

N.C. Division of Parks and Recreation
P.O. Box 100
Sapphire, NC 28774-0100
(828) 966-9099
gorges@ncmail.net
www.ncparks.gov

# green river game land

**Henderson & Polk Counties**
**18,639 acres**

## Features

The Green River Game Land is a relatively undisturbed wilderness area containing narrow gorges, steep ravines and coves, old-growth forests, and mixed hardwood forests. The Green River runs through a rugged gorge on the Blue Ridge Escarpment. At its most impressive point, the river drops 400 feet in a distance of one and a half miles and runs through a six-foot-wide crevice known as "the Narrows." Pulliam Creek cuts a deep ravine near the Green River, forming several small falls and slides.

The gorge is a very soggy area, home to the box turtle and many amphibians such as the northern dusky and blackbelly salamanders, green frog, gray treefrog, and spring peeper. The area's reptilian species include racer, ringneck, eastern garter, and black rat snakes. Many forest songbirds inhabit the gorge, including the scarlet tanager and cerulean and Swainson's warblers. Rare plants in the Green River area include butternut (white walnut), long-stalked sedge, Cherokee sedge, French Broad heartleaf, and Blue Ridge bittercress. Wildflowers such as large-flowered trillium and showy skullcap can be seen here in late spring. The gorge is also home to an uncommon butterfly, the West Virginia white. Canoeing and kayaking are popular on the Green River, so summer traffic is heavy on the lower sections.

## Conservation Highlights

The Nature Conservancy purchased 5,090 acres from Duke Power Company and Crescent Timber in 1994 on behalf of the N.C. Wildlife Resources Commission. An additional 2,699 acres has been protected with assistance from the Conservancy.

## Trip Planner

This area has multiple uses, including hunting. Downloadable maps of the game land and hunting schedules are available on the Wildlife Resources Commission web site.

There are many hiking options in the Green River area. The Environmental and Conservation Organization of Henderson County (ECO) has a nice trail map and guide. Contact them at (828) 692-0385 or on the Internet at www.eco-wnc.org.

## Ownership/Access

N.C. Wildlife Resources Commission
1 (800) 662-7137
www.ncwildlife.org

(John Warner)

# hickory nut gorge

The rocky outcroppings and cascading waterfalls of Hickory Nut Gorge make it an ecological treasure of national significance. Located just 15 miles southeast of Asheville, Hickory Nut Gorge is home to 37 rare plant species, including broadleaf coreopsis and Carey's saxifrage, while its caves provide habitat for rare salamander and endangered bat species and its steep slopes and high peaks host an array of bird species. Hickory Nut Gorge is cloaked in cove hardwood forest, with Carolina hemlock and chestnut oak forest on the cliff tops and ridgeline. The gorge is also an important habitat for table mountain pine, which is a small pine endemic to the Southern Appalachians.

from left: (The Nature Conservancy); (Bill Lea)

# bat cave preserve

**Henderson & Rutherford Counties**
**186 acres**

## Features

Bat Cave is the longest augen gneiss fissure cave in the world, with 1.23 miles of surveyed passage. Its main chamber is a dark cathedral more than 300 feet long and approximately 85 feet high. Visitors can stand in the cave entrance and feel the cool underground air flowing from deep inside the cave. Fissure caves are formed by rock splits, boulder movements, and other motions of the earth, while most other caves are formed by water dissolving and abrading rock.

While the impressive cave opening is the attraction for most visitors, the rugged slopes around Bat Cave contain an equally important array of habitats and creatures. A mature cove hardwood forest covers the rocky middle and lower slopes of the gorge, and Carolina hemlock and chestnut oak forest dominate the cliff tops and ridgeline. The cove forests harbor a number of threatened or endangered plants, such as dissected toothwort and broadleaf coreopsis, as well as an abundance of more common spring wildflowers, including bloodroot, toothwort, trillium, and violets. The rare and vibrantly colored cerulean warbler also inhabits the preserve's cove forest and two rare salamander species are found here as well.

## Conservation Highlights

In 1981, Margaret Flinsch began making gifts of undivided interest in the Bat Cave natural area to The Nature Conservancy. The area, which had been the property of the Flinsch family since 1920, is now owned by The Nature Conservancy. The preserve is managed to protect the cave entrances from winter disturbance during bat hibernating season and to control invasive species such as kudzu, tree-of-heaven, multiflora rose, wineberry, Japanese honeysuckle, and English ivy that threaten the preserve's native plants.

## Trip Planner

The cave itself is closed to visitation at all times, and the preserve is closed from late October to mid-April in an effort to allow the bats to hibernate undisturbed. If bats are disturbed during hibernation, they fly around and quickly use up the stored energy that they need to survive the winter.

During the summer, The Nature Conservancy offers field trips and guided tours of the preserve. For field trips, follow the links to field trips in North Carolina at www.nature.org. To schedule a hike during the summer season, call (828) 350-1431, or email Mtns_Volunteers@tnc.org.

The trail to Bat Cave is a mile long (one-way), with the last half mile fairly steep and strenuous. Participants in guided hikes should wear long pants and sturdy footwear and carry water. Walking sticks may also be useful.

Chimney Rock State Park and Bat Cave Preserve are within easy driving distance of Charlotte. The area is a good day trip from

Bat Cave entrance (Alan Cressler)

western North Carolina destinations such as Asheville, Hendersonville, and Pisgah Forest.

Lake Lure, which is located at the base of Chimney Rock, provides a good local base for exploring the area.

## Ownership/Access

The Nature Conservancy
P.O. Box 17519
Asheville, NC 28816
(828) 350-1431
www.nature.org/northcarolina

# rainbow falls

**Rutherford County • 162.55 acres**

## Features

The stream that feeds Rainbow Falls forms between Roaringrock Mountain and Cedar Knob and meets up with additional tributaries on the eastern edge of Bald Mountain before plunging 160 feet to the valley below, where it joins the Rocky Broad River near Chimney Rock. Rainbow Falls supports a healthy spray cliff natural community, where constant moisture, regulated temperatures, and shallow soils create a unique and diverse plant habitat rich in ferns and mosses. The slopes surrounding Rainbow Falls feature extensive chestnut oak stands, as well as oak-hickory forests that provide habitat for the rare lampshade spider, Biltmore carrionflower, and the federally listed white irisette. Timber rattlesnakes, which are very sensitive to human disturbance, have been found on the tract, indicating that it is in good ecological condition.

## Conservation Highlights

Prior owners of a portion of the Rainbow Falls property, Thomas and Miny Hebb, worked closely with The Nature Conservancy to ensure that the land would be protected for future generations, and they sold it to the Conservancy at a bargain price. This portion of the property was purchased with funds from the chapter's Forever Wild campaign.

## Trip Planner

This Nature Conservancy preserve is only accessible through the North Carolina Chapter's field trip program. Contact the North Carolina Mountains Office at (828) 350-1431 for details.

## Ownership/Access

The Nature Conservancy
P.O. Box 17519
Asheville, NC 28816
(828) 350-1431
www.nature.org/northcarolina

Rainbow Falls (The Nature Conservancy)

# rumbling bald preserve

**Buncombe & Rutherford Counties**
**1,100 acres**

## Features

One of the most prominent features in Hickory Nut Gorge, Rumbling Bald is a long mountain located on the north side of the gorge that extends from about one mile northwest of Lake Lure and links up with Shumont Mountain. Rumbling Bald is distinctive for its series of three mounds and towering rock cliffs. The mountain was known simply as Bald Mountain until 1874, when a series of earthquakes caused loud rumbling in the area—a reminder that western North Carolina still occasionally experiences noticeable earth tremors. The mountain gradually rises in elevation to about 2,800 feet and is characterized by sheer cliffs and granite domes. Mature chestnut oak forest and oak-hickory forest cover much of the mountain's slopes and crest. Rare plants, including the federally endangered white irisette, grow in these forests. A rocky outcrop on the north side of the mountain's crest supports roundleaf serviceberry, Biltmore sedge, and eastern shooting star.

Rumbling Bald is home to a wealth of unusual animals. The common raven nests in these rocky exposed cliffs. The uncommon Bat Cave form of the Yonahlossee salamander, formerly known as the crevice salamander, also inhabits this preserve. Several large fissure caves on the preserve serve as hibernation spots for many bats, including the eastern small-footed myotis.

## Conservation Highlights

The Nature Conservancy purchased 788 acres at Rumbling Bald in 2001 from Camp Lurecrest Ministries and later purchased two additional tracts, protecting 312 acres.

## Trip Planner

This Nature Conservancy preserve is only accessible through the North Carolina Chapter's field trip program. Contact the North Carolina Mountains Office at (828) 350-1431 for details.

A good alternative is to visit Chimney Rock State Park (detailed elsewhere in this guide), which provides great views of Hickory Nut Gorge and good examples of the kind of flora and fauna found at Rumbling Bald. Visitors to Lake Lure can get a good view of distinctive Rumbling Bald itself.

## Ownership/Access

The Nature Conservancy
P.O. Box 17519
Asheville, NC 28816
(828) 350-1431
www.nature.org/northcarolina

View from Rumbling Bald (Alan Cressler)

# chimney rock state park

**Rutherford County • 3,500 acres**

## Features

The most recognized part of the park is Chimney Rock—a 315-foot rock outcropping with an elevation of 2,280 feet, which provides spectacular views across Hickory Nut Gorge. The park contains 3.5 miles of trails, which range from near flat and suitable for families with small children to strenuous climbs for more experienced trekkers.

The 1,568-acre World's Edge tract contains a mile-long set of steep slopes on the eastern edge of the Blue Ridge Escarpment, with nearly four miles of streams and waterfalls. Home to many rare plant species, World's Edge also provides habitat for rare salamanders, endangered bats, peregrine falcons, flocks of songbirds migrating to and from the tropics, and a host of other native plants and animals.

Tourists have visited Chimney Rock since 1885, when the first stairway to the summit was built. Chimney Rock itself is operated by a private contractor and currently provides the only access to the park. The Division of Parks and Recreation is developing a master plan that will guide the park's future development.

## Conservation Highlights

The North Carolina General Assembly created a state park in Hickory Nut Gorge in 2005. The park was named Chimney Rock State Park after the state bought Chimney Rock Park, which had been operated as a private concern.

In 2005, The Nature Conservancy joined with the Carolina Mountain Land Conservancy to announce the $16 million acquisition of World's Edge. Loans from the Open Space Institute and the Self-Help Credit Union, as well as guarantees by the Conservation Trust for North Carolina, made the acquisition possible on a very tight timeline to prevent the tract's purchase by a developer. World's Edge is now part of Chimney Rock State Park.

The Nature Conservancy is working to fill in the gaps to protect Hickory Nut Gorge. In recent years, the Conservancy has acquired several important tracts of land in the area, including areas that protect the top of Rumbling Bald (in this guide) and much of nearby Roundtop Mountain, as well as forested buffer that protects nearby Bat Cave Preserve (detailed in this guide). In future years, it is likely that these acquisitions will be transferred to the state as part of Chimney Rock State Park.

The acquisition of these tracts is part of a far-reaching conservation strategy for important natural resources in the gorge and for the development of Chimney Rock State Park. The Nature Conservancy, along with its partners, the Foothills Conservancy of North Carolina and the Carolina Mountain Land Conservancy, is working to acquire additional property that will also be transferred to the state park system.

Chimney Rock (The Nature Conservancy)

## Trip Planner

As of 2008, Chimney Rock State Park provides the only public access to Hickory Nut Gorge. About 3,500 acres have been set aside for the park, but only a thousand acres are currently accessible to the public. The N.C. Division of Parks and Recreation will develop a master plan for the park, which will guide future access at the site.

At press time the N.C. Division of Parks and Recreation had signed a contract that will allow park visitors to make advance registration for campsites, shelters, and other facilities via a toll-free number and online. The system should be functional by summer 2009 and information will be posted on the park web site at www.ncparks.gov.

## Ownership/Access

N.C. Division of Parks and Recreation
P.O. Box 220
Chimney Rock, NC 28720
(828) 625-1823
chimney.rock@ncmail.net
www.ncparks.gov

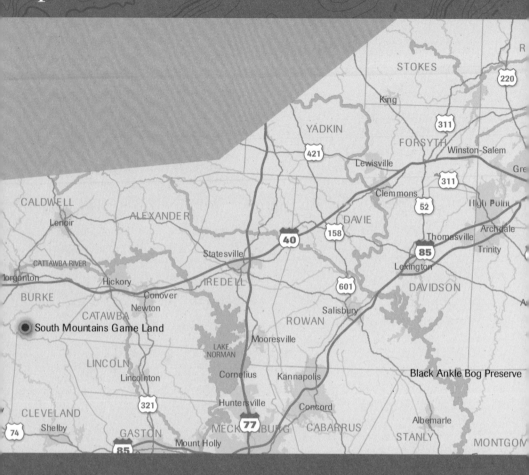

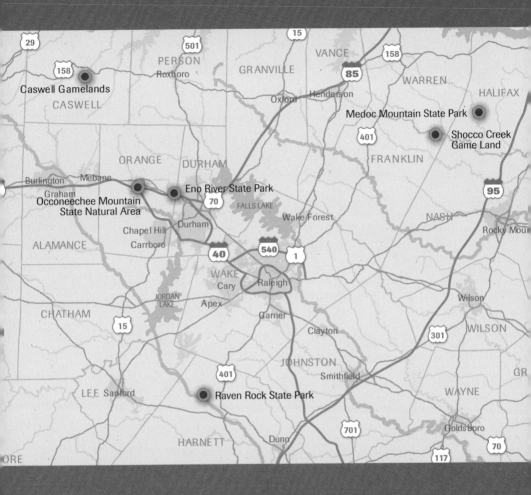

Caswell Gamelands

Medoc Mountain State Park

Shocco Creek Game Land

Eno River State Park

Occoneechee Mountain State Natural Area

Raven Rock State Park

# piedmont landscape

Cedar Waxwing (Ida Phillips)

North Carolina's Piedmont extends from the fall line east of Raleigh to the first high peaks of the Southern Appalachian Mountains more than 250 miles to the west. Working in both the rural countryside and major urban areas, The Nature Conservancy has a long history of conservation in the Piedmont.

The low foothills and rich soils of the Piedmont have always appealed to humans; today, well over half of North Carolina's 8.5 million residents live here. But human communities aren't the only ones that thrive in the middle of our state.

The Piedmont supports a wide range of natural habitats, which shelter a diversity of wildlife. The region's hardwood forests are home to white-tailed deer and wild turkey. Rare Piedmont prairies explode every spring and summer with native wildflowers. And fast moving streams and rivers host nationally significant populations of fish and mussels.

Given the extensive and dense human habitation in the Piedmont, The Nature Conservancy's work in this region tends to involve publicly accessible land. Conservancy projects here range from Eno River and Raven Rock State Parks to state game lands at Shocco Creek and the South Mountains. The Conservancy works with local and state partners to preserve the natural diversity of the Piedmont.

Piedmont mesic hardwoods (Mike Schafale)

# south mountains game land

**Burke, Cleveland, McDowell, &
Rutherford Counties • 19,775 acres**

## Features

The rugged South Mountains range is a reminder of the wilderness that once characterized North Carolina's Piedmont. The mountains rise abruptly over the landscape near Morganton, reaching elevations of almost 3,000 feet. This large block of unfragmented forest straddles several counties. The South Mountains Game Land, formerly known as the Rollins Tract, spans more than 14 miles along the spine of the mountain range and borders the 12,725-acre South Mountains State Park.

The N.C. Natural Heritage Program considers the South Mountains to have national biological significance. The land harbors many rare natural communities, including rocky summits, rich cove forests, and old-growth forests. The property is home to wildlife species such as black bear, bobcat, mink, brook trout, and migratory songbirds. Twenty-two rare plant species thrive in the South Mountains, including one of North America's rarest orchids—the small whorled pogonia.

The game land contains the headwaters of the First Broad River, which supply the city of Shelby and upper Cleveland County water systems.

## Conservation Highlights

A partnership of public and private conservation groups, including The Nature Conservancy, the Foothills Conservancy of North Carolina, and the N.C. Wildlife Resources Commission, worked for four years to acquire the Rollins Tract and establish the South Mountains Game Land. In 1998, The Nature Conservancy purchased the tract for $13.4 million from the McDonald Investment Corporation and transferred the property to the N.C. Wildlife Resources Commission. The Foothills Conservancy of North Carolina, a regional land trust, played a decisive role in this victory for landscape-level conservation.

## Trip Planner

This area has multiple uses, including hunting. Downloadable maps of the game land and hunting schedules are available on the Wildlife Resources Commission web site.

You can also visit South Mountains State Park, adjacent to the game land. The park offers hiking trails, bridle trails, and camping. The park is located 18 miles south of Morganton. Leave I-40 at exit 105, and take NC 18 south about 10 miles. Turn right on Sugar Loaf Road (SR 1913), go four miles, turn left, and take SR 1924 for two miles. Turn right on SR 1901 and drive 1.5 miles, then turn right onto SR 1904 and drive 3.6 miles to the park entrance.

## Ownership/Access

N.C. Wildlife Resources Commission
1 (800) 662-7137
www.ncwildlife.org

Red maple in fall (Jodie LaPoint)

# black ankle bog preserve

**Montgomery County • 284 acres**

## Features

Walking from the forested ridges of this preserve down into the stream heads that contain one of the few remaining Piedmont bogs, the vegetation shifts from plant communities requiring dry conditions, such as longleaf pine and the chestnut oak woodlands common to the nearby Uwharrie Mountains, to the treeless areas of the bog community. Blackjack oak, post oak, and dense huckleberry and blueberry shrubs surround mats of sphagnum moss and patches of habenaria orchid, milkwort, sedges, cinnamon fern, and trumpet and purple pitcher plants. Downhill from the bog the habitat blends into a dense thicket dominated by alder, sweet bay, sweet pepperbush, Virginia sweetspire, and the endangered bog spicebush that grows in these low areas.

A patch of climbing fern, a large stand of sweetleaf, and the rare large witch-alder also grow in the preserve. Birds such as wild turkey, hairy and pileated woodpeckers, and broad-winged hawk, which are commonly found on large tracts of unbroken woodlands, also inhabit Black Ankle Bog.

The preserve contains scattered longleaf pines, reminders of the trees that were once prevalent in this area on the border between the Coastal Plain and the Piedmont. Apparently the name Black Ankle was inspired by the sight of someone walking through the area after one of the frequent fires that occurred here historically.

## Conservation Highlights

The North Carolina Chapter purchased this tract in 1991 from the Dassow Property Corporation. For the next 20 to 25 years, The Nature Conservancy will continue to restore the preserve to its historic condition by conducting controlled burns and planting longleaf pine seedlings grown from local seed sources. The North Carolina Zoo, U.S. Fish and Wildlife Service, and N.C. Division of Forest Resources are actively supporting The Nature Conservancy in this restoration effort.

## Trip Planner

This Nature Conservancy preserve is only accessible through the North Carolina Chapter's field trip program. For more information, call (919) 403-8558.

## Ownership/Access

The Nature Conservancy
4705 University Drive, Suite 290
Durham, NC 27707
(919) 403-8558
www.nature.org/northcarolina

Glade with pitcher plants (Margit Bucher)

# caswell game land

**Caswell County • 17,198 acres**

## Features

Caswell Game Land resembles a North Carolina Piedmont forest prior to European settlement, as it protects a large expanse of upland hardwood forest interspersed with pine forest. Although isolated patches of upland forest are scattered through the Piedmont, Caswell Game Land protects one of the state's most extensive examples of this forest type.

In the early 1900s, this property was divided into small farms and the ridgetops were cleared for fields. Years of intensive farming and the economic hardship of the Depression forced many of the landowners to sell out, and the property eventually transferred into government hands. The area's dissected topography contains a mixture of rolling hills, steep ravines, and mostly narrow, flat ridges. Oak-hickory forest dominates most of the area and grows on the upper and mid-level slopes and ridgetops. Two large creeks run through the area and the bottomland forests dominate the stream banks.

This extensive forested block provides an important habitat for wide-ranging wildlife. Neotropical migratory birds, including wood thrush, scarlet tanager, and ovenbird, breed in the game land. The game land is most noteworthy for supporting one of the state's largest wild turkey populations.

## Conservation Highlights

The federal government purchased much of this land in the 1930s and eventually transferred it to the U.S. Forest Service, which sold the property in 1959 to the N.C. Wildlife Resources Commission. The Nature Conservancy purchased tracts in 1999 and 2007, totaling 539 acres, which were transferred to the game land.

## Trip Planner

Caswell Game Land is located south of Yanceyville on both sides of NC 62. You can walk into the game land on the gated dirt roads off NC 62. This area has multiple uses, including hunting. Downloadable maps of the game land and hunting schedules are available on the Wildlife Resources Commission web site.

## Ownership/Access

N.C. Wildlife Resources Commission
1 (800) 662-7137
www.ncwildlife.org

Turtle (Bill Lea)

# occoneechee mountain state natural area

**Orange County • 190 acres**

## Features

Occoneechee Mountain is the highest point in Orange County at 867 feet. There is no point higher between Hillsborough and the Atlantic Ocean. Visitors to Occoneechee Mountain might think they are in the mountains of western North Carolina, because the ridge and its northern slopes feature plants that are typically found in the mountains.

Occoneechee's northern slope, which rises 350 feet above the Eno River, is relatively cool and moist. At the end of the ice age, it became a refuge for a number of mountain species. Catawba rhododendron, mountain laurel, galax, Bradley's spleenwort, mountain spleenwort, climbing fern, and wild sarsaparilla all grow here. Rare species include sweet pinesap, large witch-alder, and the purple fringeless orchid. A special resident is the brown elfin butterfly, another mountain species—the next closest brown elfin butterflies are found 100 miles to the west of Hillsborough.

The mountain gets its name from the Occaneechi Indian tribe. In the 1600s the tribe moved from present-day Clarksville, Virginia, to a home on the Eno River less than two miles from Occoneechee Mountain. Descendants of the tribe still live in the area.

Hillsborough was a colonial town, and the area was subdivided numerous times over the years. Until the mid-20th century, a mill village was housed on part of what is now Occoneechee Mountain State Natural Area.

Despite all the activity in the area, Occoneechee Mountain stayed wild; the last surviving panther in this part of the Piedmont lived on Occoneechee. The Panther's Den ravine is one of the most significant areas on the mountain, extending from the river bottomland to roughly 700 feet on the north-facing slope. The ravine is constantly shaded, creating a damp, cool microhabitat for mountain species.

## Conservation Highlights

The mountain was saved due to the efforts of several dedicated individuals, the Eno River Association, and The Nature Conservancy. A local couple, Allen and Pauline Lloyd, kicked off those conservation efforts in the early 1960s when they bought and saved 66 acres on the west side of the mountain shortly after a mining operation opened on the eastern side. In 1987, Cone Mills donated 28 acres to the town of Hillsborough. In 1997 and 1998, The Nature Conservancy purchased an additional 96 acres. The Occoneechee Mountain State Natural Area was dedicated in 1999 and is managed as part of the Eno River State Park, which is detailed elsewhere in this guide.

## Trip Planner

To reach Occoneechee Mountain State Natural Area from I-85, take exit 164, turning north on Churton Street toward downtown Hillsborough. Turn left at the next traffic light onto Mayo Street. At the next stop sign, turn left onto Orange Grove Road. Turn at the

Occoneechee woods (George Sagar)

second right on to Virginia Cates Road, just before the bridge under the interstate, and follow the signs to the parking area.

The park has several nice, easy loop trails with good views of the Eno River; follow the signs to those trails. The best view is from one of the loop trails, atop a Civil War–era quarry, overlooking the Eno River. Restrooms and picnic tables are available at the parking lot.

## Ownership/Access

North Carolina Division of Parks and Recreation
6101 Cole Mill Road
Durham, NC 27705-9275
(919) 383-1686
eno.river@ncmail.net
www.ncparks.gov

# eno river state park

**Durham & Orange Counties**
**2,635 acres**

## Features

A quick drive north from Durham and Chapel Hill will bring you to a great hiking spot, Eno River State Park. The Eno River flows east from Orange County into Durham County and eventually joins the Little and Flat Rivers and becomes the Neuse River. Adjacent to centers of extensive development, the park retains many of the natural features that once prevailed in the Piedmont, including various second-growth Piedmont forest communities: dry pine heath, mixed upland hardwoods, moist hardwoods, and floodplain forest. Ancient Native American settlements and mills from the 18th and 19th centuries located along the river illustrate the human history of the region.

The river and its floodplain harbor beaver, river otter, mink, and muskrat, as well as wood duck, great blue heron, and spotted sandpiper. The high-quality river supports large populations of freshwater mussels, crayfish, numerous fish species, and aquatic invertebrates. The hardwood forests are home to wild turkey and many migratory songbirds.

The park is divided into three separate sections; Few's Ford is the principal visitor access point to the park office and interpretive exhibits. There are several canoe access points within the park. Canoeing is good during the winter and spring, when the river is between one and three feet deep.

The park is a good place to visit throughout the year. In March, before the trees have leafed out, the floodplain is rich in spring ephemeral wildflowers. Early April brings migrating warblers and a great variety of wildflowers. Mountain laurel and Catawba rhododendron bloom in early to mid-May. The pump station area contains a good example of a beech-dominated Piedmont forest with a rich understory including yellow lady's slipper and showy orchis.

## Conservation Highlights

Since 1971, The Nature Conservancy, in cooperation with the Association for the Preservation of the Eno River Valley and the N.C. Division of Parks and Recreation, has protected 667 acres of what is now part of Eno River State Park from threats of logging and development. In 1997 and 1998, the Conservancy acquired 97 acres at Occoneechee Mountain near Hillsborough that are now owned and managed by Eno River State Park as part of a State Natural Area. Occoneechee Mountain is also described in this guide.

## Trip Planner

A good place to begin a visit to Eno River State Park is at the visitor center at the Few's Ford section of the park, where you can pick up maps and brochures. Going west from Durham on I-85 (South), take exit 170 to US 70 West. Drive 0.2 mile and turn right at the brown state park sign onto Pleasant Green Road. After about two miles, turn left onto Cole Mill Road and drive a mile to the park entrance.

Fisherman on Eno River (Jodie LaPoint)

At press time the N.C. Division of Parks and Recreation had signed a contract that will allow park visitors to make advance registration for campsites, shelters, and other facilities via a toll-free number and online. The system should be functional by summer 2009, and information will be posted on the park web site at www.ncparks.gov.

## Ownership/Access

6101 Cole Mill Road
Durham, NC 27705-9275
(919) 383-1686
eno.river@ncmail.net
www.ncparks.gov

# raven rock state park

## Features

Raven Rock State Park is a great destination for folks in the Triangle or Fayetteville areas who are looking for a getaway spot for hiking, camping, or canoeing. Bordering four miles of the Cape Fear River near the town of Lillington, the park offers scenic Piedmont woodland communities and paddling opportunities.

The river divides the park into two sections: the southern section is more rugged and contains high bluffs on the riverbanks, while the northern section contains a low, flat flood plain. Raven Rock itself is a steep quartzite bluff on the south side of the river that rises 150 feet over the waterway. Over time, the river has undercut the banks, creating the highest bluff along the North Carolina fall line (the junction between the Piedmont and the Coastal Plain regions). According to local lore, ravens once roosted on the rocky ledges, but the species is no longer present in the eastern half of the state.

A variety of forest types are found in the park. The flood plain forest contains sycamore and river birch. Oak-hickory forests and pine forests dominate the upland ridges and the top of the bluffs, while mixed hardwood forests grow on the sheltered slopes. The park also contains a remnant longleaf pine forest. In early spring, wildflowers such as spring beauty, Solomon's seal, and the locally rare Dutchman's breeches cover the forest floor. Buttercup phacelia, an herb found in only a few river floodplains east of the Appalachians, is abundant in the park. In late spring, rhododendron and mountain laurel thickets bloom along the bluffs.

Raven Rock State Park supports elusive animals such as the fox squirrel, gray fox, and muskrat. The park also provides habitat for many species of salamanders and frogs, such as slimy salamander and southern leopard frog. There are over 160 species of birds including wild turkey, wood duck, hawks, owl, and migratory song birds that breed in the park during spring and summer.

## Conservation Highlights

The State of North Carolina established Raven Rock State Park in 1969. The state purchased more than 221 acres of land in 1970 and later received a donation of 170 acres from Burlington Industries. The state has acquired additional land since that time, including a 128-acre tract purchased by The Nature Conservancy in 1999.

## Trip Planner

The park is located nine miles west of Lillington and 20 miles east of Sanford. Turn north off of US 421 and follow Raven Rock Road (SR 1314) for three miles to the park. The northern section of the park can be accessed from US 401 between Lillington and Kipling by SR 1412 and SR 1418.

The park has a number of hiking trails, including the one-mile Raven Rock Loop Trail, which will take the trekker to the base of Raven Rock. There are also seven miles of

Anemone (Mike Schafale)

horseback trails. A portion of the Cape Fear Canoe Trail runs through the park. There is no access point to the trail inside the park, but rangers can give you details about how to access the trail. Once inside the park, signs point to canoe camping in the park. There are also backpack camping opportunities in the park, including group sites that can hold up to 20 people. Anglers can take advantage of healthy populations of game fish such as largemouth bass, warmouth, bluegill, catfish redear, and green sunfish.

At press time the N.C. Division of Parks and Recreation had signed a contract that will allow park visitors to make advance registration for campsites, shelters, and other facilities via a toll-free number and online. The system should be functional by summer 2009, and information will be posted on the park web site, www.ncparks.gov.

## Ownership/Access

N.C. Division of Parks and Recreation
3000 Raven Rock Road
Lillington, NC 27546
(910) 893-4888
info.ravenrock@ncmail.net
www.ncparks.gov

White-tailed deer (Jodie LaPoint); Turkey (Bill Lea)

THE TAR BEGINS AS A FRESHWATER STREAM NEAR ROXBORO, NOT FAR FROM THE VIRGINIA BORDER. At Washington, the river becomes brackish and its name changes to Pamlico. Eventually, it flows into Pamlico Sound.

The rich aquatic diversity found in the Tar River watershed is one of the major reasons The Nature Conservancy became involved in preserving land in the area.

Most of The Nature Conservancy's work in North Carolina has been in the Upper Tar River area. The Upper Tar has exceptional biological richness in its aquatic communities, including several species of freshwater mussel and more than 60 species of freshwater fish.

The Tar is home to 12 rare freshwater mussels. Its watershed provides critical habitat for the federally endangered Tar River spinymussel. Most freshwater mussels have smooth shells—the Tar River spinymussel is one of only three that have spines on their shells.

In 2006, The Nature Conservancy acquired nearly 220,000 acres of forestland across 10 states from International Paper Company. This was the single largest private land conservation sale in the history of the South, and one of the largest in the nation. Most of that land was added to game lands and to Medoc Mountain State Park, ensuring public access and at the same time preserving high water quality.

Upper Tar River (The Nature Conservancy)

# shocco creek game land

**Franklin, Halifax, Nash, & Warren Counties • 29,639 acres**

## Features

Shocco Creek is home to a number of mussels, including the federally endangered dwarf wedge mussel and the notched rainbow mussel. Wild turkey, neotropical migratory birds, and wood ducks are also found in the area.

The game land has become well known as a place to see butterflies; as many as 25 different species have been recorded during a single field trip. Dragonflies are also numerous. The best place to see butterflies and dragonflies is along power line clearings and close to the water.

## Conservation Highlights

In March 2006, The Nature Conservancy, International Paper, and The Conservation Fund announced an agreement to protect nearly 220,000 acres of forestland across 10 states. This was the single largest private land conservation sale in the history of the South, and one of the largest in the nation. As part of this deal, The Nature Conservancy purchased and transferred 21,682 acres to the N.C. Wildlife Resources Commission for inclusion in the Shocco Creek Game Land.

## Trip Planner

Remember, this area has multiple uses, including hunting. Downloadable maps of the game land and hunting schedules are available on the Wildlife Resources Commission web site.

Since Shocco Creek Game Land is scattered across several counties, directions are best obtained from the Wildlife Resources Commission's downloadable maps.

Toad (Ida Phillips)

## Ownership/Access

N.C. Wildlife Resources Commission
1 (800) 662-7137
www.ncwildlife.org

(The Nature Conservancy)

**Halifax County • 3,807 acres**

## Conservation Highlights

In 2006, The Nature Conservancy acquired nearly 220,000 acres of forestland across 10 states from International Paper Company. This was, at the time, the single largest private land conservation sale in the history of the South, and one of the largest in the nation. As part of this deal, The Nature Conservancy purchased and transferred 1,507 acres to the N.C. Division of Parks and Recreation for inclusion in the park.

## Trip Planner

Medoc Mountain State Park offers a wide array of recreational opportunities, all just a 90-minute drive from Research Triangle Park.

Tent, trailer, and group camping for parties as large as 35 individuals are available. Facilities include picnic tables and grills. The large picnic shelter includes a fireplace and a drinking fountain.

Recreational activities abound. There are more than 12 miles of hiking trails, most of which are relatively moderate and suitable for families with children. Anglers can try their luck at reeling in blue gill, large mouth bass, redbreast sunfish, Roanoke bass, and chain pickerel. You can also put your canoe in the waters of Little Fishing Creek, which is accessible from the SR 1322 bridge. Canoeists putting in there can take a leisurely two-hour trip to a take-out point at the SR 1002 bridge.

Off I-95, take exit 160 at NC 561 west and travel nine miles to the park. Turn left on SR 1322, which will bring you to the park office, on the right.

## Features

The highest point at Medoc is 325 feet above sea level, all that's left of a mountain range that was formed by volcanoes during the Paleozoic Era. Visitors will notice that Medoc's rugged terrain looks nothing like other nearby lowlands. Over the years, Medoc Mountain has resisted the erosion that characterized the surrounding area. Medoc Mountain has extreme slopes on its north and west sides, with the elevation dropping 160 feet in a quarter of a mile. Little Fishing Creek meanders through the park, creating a beautiful landscape.

Medoc Mountain is home to mountain laurel; a rare find this far from western North Carolina. American beech, which is more common in highlands, is also found at Medoc. The park also houses the southern flying squirrel, gray fox, river otter, beaver, and muskrat. A rare large salamander, the Carolina mudpuppy, is found in the area.

Over the years, the area was heavily farmed. One of its early farmers was Sidney Weller, who grew grapes in the area, producing a wine known as Weller's Halifax. Weller is considered to be the father of American winemaking. He named the mountain Medoc after the French province of Bordeaux, which is well known for its wines. The area was timbered in the 1930s. Today, the N.C. Division of Parks and Recreation is restoring the area to its original forested state.

(The Nature Conservancy)

## Ownership/Access

N.C. Division of Parks and Recreation
1541 Medoc State Park Road
Hollister, NC 27844
(252) 586-6588
medoc.mountain@ncmail.net
www.ncparks.gov

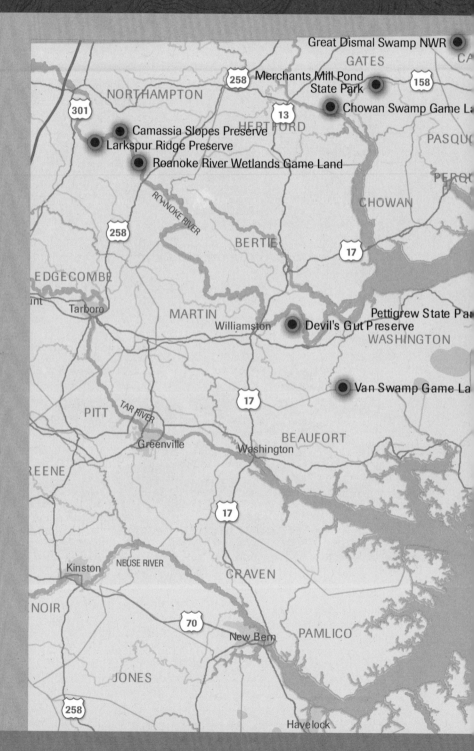

Great Dismal Swamp NWR

GATES

CA

258

Merchants Mill Pond
State Park

158

NORTHAMPTON

13

Chowan Swamp Game La

301

HERTFORD

PASQUO

Camassia Slopes Preserve

Larkspur Ridge Preserve

Roanoke River Wetlands Game Land

CHOWAN

ROANOKE RIVER

258

BERTIE

17

EDGECOMBE

int

Tarboro

MARTIN

Williamston

Devil's Gut Preserve

Pettigrew State Par

WASHINGTON

PITT

TAR RIVER

17

Van Swamp Game La

Greenville

Washington

BEAUFORT

REENE

17

Kinston

NEUSE RIVER

CRAVEN

NOIR

70

New Bern

PAMLICO

JONES

258

Havelock

Northwest River Marsh Game Land

URRITUCK

Currituck Banks

North River Game Land

eth City

Kitty Hawk Woods Coastal Reserve

BEMARLE SOUND

Nags Head Woods Preserve

Jockey's Ridge State Park

64   Manteo

Alligator River NWR

DARE

LL

264

OE

AMUSKEET

Swanquarter NWR

PAMLICO SOUND

Buxton Woods

Cape Lookout National Seashore

dar Island NWR

Albemarle
ANLY
MONTGOMERY
MOORE
HARNETT
Dunn
PEE DEE RIVER
52
15
Pinehurst
Long Valley Farm
Spring Lake
Carvers Creek State Pa
Sandhills
Game Land
Weymouth Woods
Nature Preserve
95
ANSON
Calloway Sandhills Preserve
RICHMOND
Fayetteville
CUMBERLAND
SAMPS
HOKE
Rockingham
Hope Mills
Pondberry Bay
Hamlet
SCOTLAND
15
301
Horseshoe La
Carolina Bay Preserves
Laurinburg
South River Prese
ROBESON
Lumberton
BLADEN
95
301
LUMBER RIVER
Lumber River State Park
76
74
Lake Waccamaw State Park
COLUMBUS
Old Dock Savanna Preserve
Myrtle Head Savanna Preserve
Columbus County Game Land

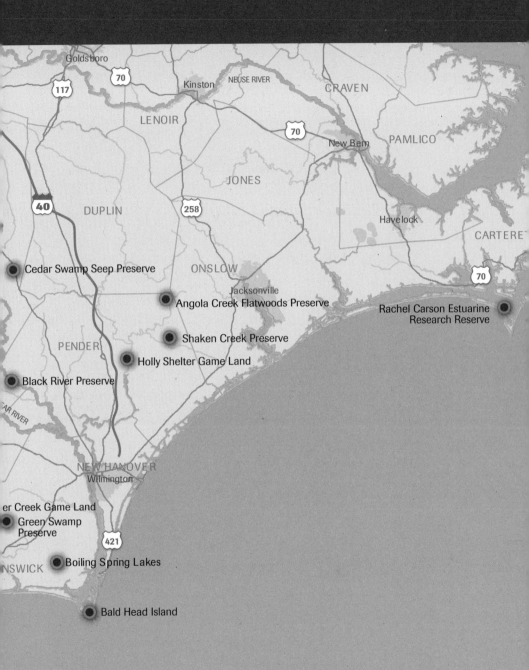

Goldsboro

70

117

Kinston      NEUSE RIVER      CRAVEN

LENOIR

70      New Bern      PAMLICO

40      DUPLIN      JONES      258

Havelock

CARTERE

ONSLOW

70

Cedar Swamp Seep Preserve

Jacksonville

Angola Creek Flatwoods Preserve      Rachel Carson Estuarine
Research Reserve

Shaken Creek Preserve

PENDER      Holly Shelter Game Land

Black River Preserve

AR RIVER

NEW HANOVER
Wilmington

er Creek Game Land
Green Swamp
Preserve

421

NSWICK      Boiling Spring Lakes

Bald Head Island

# the coastal plain

from left: (John Warner); Alligator River (Debbie Crane)

Norra Carolina's Coastal Plain runs from Virginia to South Carolina and extends inward almost to Raleigh, where the land begins to rise imperceptibly into the Piedmont. The Nature Conservancy has worked in the Coastal Plain for three decades to protect the unique natural communities that thrive here.

The region's numerous rivers, streams, and wetlands are the lifeblood of the Coastal Plain, providing rich habitat for plants and animals, soaking up floodwaters, and feeding North Carolina's sounds and bays.

In these low-lying areas, a rise of mere inches in elevation can bring a host of different species and habitat types. The Coastal Plain has some of the richest biodiversity found anywhere in the world, supporting an extraordinary range of plant life. Rare animals like the red-cockaded woodpecker make this place home, as do more familiar creatures like the black bear, the bald

eagle, and the American alligator.

The Coastal Plain is the site of some of the Conservancy's most recognized North Carolina projects, from the floodplain forests of the Roanoke River and the longleaf savannas of the Green Swamp to the many state parks and national wildlife refuges that dot the region. The Nature Conservancy works with partners ranging from private landowners and local communities to the U.S. military and a host of state agencies to protect

the natural treasures of this unique landscape.

In 2007, The Nature Conservancy reached a major milestone in the Coastal Plain—protection of the entire 70-mile shoreline of the Alligator River. This completes almost three decades of conservation efforts to protect the Alligator River and surrounding lands. Much of that shoreline lies in game lands or wildlife refuges that are accessible to the public.

# chowan swamp game land

**Bertie, Gates, & Hertford Counties**
**27,516 acres**

## Features

One of the most extensive swamp forests in North Carolina, Chowan Swamp averages three miles in width and is characterized by a diversity of natural communities. Most of the game land consists of nonriverine swamp forest. Swamp tupelo and red maple dominate the forest, while bald cypress and water tupelo are confined to a narrow strip along the river. The forests growing on the narrow upland ridges within the swamp range from mixed hardwood forest, composed of beech and a variety of oak species, to pine—oak scrub similar to that of the Chowan Sand Banks.

The mouths of Bennett's, Sarem, and Catherine Creeks are distinguished by their highly diverse freshwater marshes, containing large patches of prairie cordgrass, a significantly rare species in North Carolina, as well as wild rice and arrow arum. The Chowan is home to many breeding neotropical migrants such as prothonotary and Swainson's warblers and mammals such as black bear, bobcat, and river otter.

## Conservation Highlights

Between 1973 and 1994, The Nature Conservancy worked with Union Camp Corporation and Georgia-Pacific Corporation to protect almost 10,966 acres, which was then transferred to the N.C. Wildlife Resources Commission.

In 2006, The Nature Conservancy acquired nearly 220,000 acres of forestland across 10 states from International Paper Company. This was the single largest private land conservation sale in the history of the South, and one of the largest in the nation. As part of that deal, the Conservancy purchased 15,464 acres from IP, which were later transferred to the Wildlife Resources Commission for inclusion in the Chowan Swamp Game Land.

## Trip Planner

This area has multiple uses, including hunting. Downloadable maps of the game land and hunting schedules are available on the Wildlife Resources Commission web site.

This area is best explored by boat. A public boat ramp located at the end of New Ferry Road (SR 1111), south of Gatesville, offers the best boat access to the river.

## Ownership/Access

N.C. Wildlife Resources Commission
1 (800) 662-7137
www.ncwildlife.org

(Jodie LaPoint)

**Gates County • 3,250 acres**

## Features

The settlers who dammed Merchants Millpond before the Civil War could not have predicted that one day their efforts would result in a significant natural area. Since beavers were extirpated in North Carolina by 1900 and have only recently made a comeback, there are few old beaver ponds in the state. The 760-acre Merchants Millpond fills this niche, as over time it has developed into a mature wetland habitat supporting abundant wildlife and an old-growth forest.

The park is home to owls, woodpeckers, and waterfowl, as well as breeding neotropical migrants such as northern parula and prothonotary and yellow-throated warblers. Turtles, frogs, and snakes can be seen basking on logs and stumps. Over 200 species of birds have been observed at the park. Some of the park's more elusive inhabitants include river otter, gray fox, black bear, and bobcat. The park also provides good fishing opportunities for largemouth bass, bluegill, chain pickerel, and black crappie.

Lassiter Swamp, located in the upper end of the millpond, contains a large grove of 800-year-old cypress and the state's largest tupelo tree. The pond is bordered by a swamp forest, an old-growth beech slope, and mature mixed oak and pine stands on the uplands. Over 165 plant species have been recorded at the pond and surrounding swamp, including

the rare featherfoil or water violet (one of the odder-looking plants in the world), yellow water crowfoot, pale mannagrass, conferva pondweed, and least trillium. Green mats of waterlilies and collections of knobby cypress knees break the smooth surface of black water.

## Conservation Highlights

The park came into being in 1973 when A. B. Coleman of Moyock donated 919 acres to the N.C. Division of Parks and Recreation. That same year, The Nature Conservancy transferred 1,131 acres to the park.

## Trip Planner

This watery wilderness is best explored by canoe or kayak. You can either rent a canoe at the park or bring your own. A boat ramp and pier are located near the parking area. Follow the marked canoe trail from the boat ramp to canoe campsites. A primitive campsite on an island in the pond offers spaces for canoe-camping and there is also a campground on the uplands around the pond. Hiking trailheads are located near the entrance to the park; the park has nine miles of hiking trails. Visitors should be aware that the area is tick-laden in the summer. If you plan on hiking, you should wear long pants and a long-sleeved shirt to prevent tick bites. Be sure to check often for ticks.

The park is located six miles northeast of Gatesville. The park entrance is on NC 158, between the towns of Easons Crossroads and Sunbury, 4.8 miles west of the junction with

Cedars and Spanish moss (Jodie LaPoint)

US 32. To get to the millpond and canoe launch area from the main park entrance, drive west on US 158 for .3 miles, turn left on Millpond Road (SR 1403), and drive 1.4 miles to the parking lot on the left.

## Ownership/Access

N.C. Division of Parks and Recreation
Merchants Millpond State Park
71 US Highway 158E
Gatesville, NC 27938-9440
(252) 357-1191
merchants.millpond@ncmail.net
www.ncparks.gov

**Camden, Gates, & Pasquotank Counties
38,000 acres**

200 species, with 34 warblers and 96 nesting species. The refuge is also a haven for a number of plants, including orchids, cinnamon ferns, silky camellia, pawpaw, blackgum, and devil's walking stick.

## Features

Before European settlement, the Great Dismal Swamp covered up to 2,000 square miles. Now reduced to about 166 square miles, it is still one of the largest protected swamp wildernesses in the eastern United States. The bulk of the swamp—82,000 acres—is in Virginia, with about 38,000 acres in North Carolina.

In 1763, George Washington created the Dismal Swamp Land Company, which drained and logged large portions of the swamp. A ditch on the west side of the swamp is named after Washington. Logging in the swamp continued until 1976. Its forests once sheltered runaway slaves; in 2003, the Great Dismal Swamp was officially proclaimed a link in the "Underground Railroad Network to Freedom" for its role in provide refuge for slaves.

The area was once forested in Atlantic white cedar, cypress, and gum forest, but it was ditched, drained, and logged. The swamp is now dominated by second-growth trees and the cypress, gum, and Atlantic white cedar are found only in isolated stands. In spite of having been drastically altered by people, the Great Dismal is still a wild area where natural forces are making a comeback.

The swamp is home to a wide variety of reptiles and amphibians, and a diversity of mammals, including black bear, bobcat, river otter, mink, gray and red foxes, and several bat species. The refuge's bird list stands at over

## Conservation Highlights

In 1973, Union Camp Corporation donated 49,079 acres of the swamp in Virginia to The Nature Conservancy, which transferred the land to the Department of Interior.

Weyerhaeuser Corporation donated 10,326 acres of Dismal Swamp land to the North Carolina Chapter of The Nature Conservancy in the 1970s, and the Conservancy then transferred the land to the U.S. Fish and Wildlife Service. The Conservancy has also purchased land at the swamp from Georgia-Pacific Corporation and transferred that land to the Department of the Interior.

## Trip Planner

April, May, and June are a great time to see nesting songbirds, but summer can be oppressively hot and insect-ridden.

Camping is prohibited in the refuge, and there are no picnic tables or cooking facilities. But the park has a variety of unpaved roads that offer good walking or biking. One of the most interesting of those is the Washington Ditch Trail; the trailhead for the four-and-a-half-mile trail is near the Washington Ditch parking area. Dismal Town Boardwalk—a mile-long elevated trail that goes through the swamp—is easily accessed from the Washington Ditch Trail.

The Dismal Swamp Canal Visitor Center is the easiest access point for this area in North Carolina. The center is approximately three miles south of the North Carolina/Virginia state line on US 17. If you boat along the Dismal Swamp Canal to the visitor center, it is approximately five miles north of the South Mills Locks. Here you can learn about the commercial history of the oldest continually operating canal in the United States.

The Albemarle Region Canoe Trail system has a canoe trail on the Upper Pasquotank River that offers access into the swamp. You can access the trail at the US 17 bridge crossing southeast of Morgans Corner. You can tour Lake Drummond and some of the canals by canoe or kayak. The U.S. Fish and Wildlife Service maintains a trail for hiking and biking.

From Suffolk, Virginia, you can reach the refuge headquarters and main access points by traveling south on US 13 and VA 32 about 4.5 miles and then following the signs to the refuge. To reach Dismal Town Boardwalk Trail, take White Marsh Road (VA 642) to the Washington Ditch refuge entrance. Canoes and small boats can access 3,000-acre Lake Drummond by a feeder ditch from US 17 and the Dismal Swamp Canal on the east side of the refuge. US 158 skirts the southern border of the refuge.

The park hosts hunting days for white-tailed deer and black bear. On those days, parts of the park may be closed to other activities. A hunting schedule is available on line at www.fws.gov/northeast/greatdismalswamp/Hunting7-15-8.htm.

Gray fox (Bill Lea)

## Ownership/Access

U.S. Fish and Wildlife Service
P.O. Box 349
Suffolk, VA 23439-0349
(757) 986-3705
www.fws.gov/northeast/greatdismalswamp

**Currituck County • 3,045 acres**

## Features

The nationally significant Northwest River Marsh Game Land comprises a tranquil landscape of freshwater marsh and unusual wetlands tucked away in the far northeastern corner of North Carolina, just below the Virginia line. The Northwest River and the North Landing River flow from southeastern Virginia into northern Currituck County, where they meet and meld into the northern arm of Currituck Sound. Extensive freshwater to slightly brackish marshes fringe the rivers, along with white cedar forests and pocosins.

The freshwater marshes along the North Landing River, called Gibbs Point, are typical of much of the marsh habitat along Currituck Sound, containing taller vegetation along the river and channels and shorter vegetation in the interior. Big cordgrass, sawgrass, and broad-leaf cattail are prominent plants along the shoreline. Unfortunately, the invasive common reed has invaded the area.

Freshwater marshes are uncommon in North Carolina and provide habitat for numerous plant and animal species, as well as nurseries for fish and shellfish. Gibbs Point also has a diverse breeding bird population that includes king rail, least bittern, marsh wren, black duck, and common yellowthroat. Bald eagles forage in the area. Black bear and neotropical migratory songbirds inhabit the swamp forests in the natural area.

The marshes offer paddlers the chance to see some unusual sights, such as the Nellie Bell Ponds (several natural ponds in the middle of the marsh) and marsh cryngo, a plant that colors the marsh with a pale blue tinge when it blooms in the late summer. Waterfowl, such as black duck and snow goose, feed and rest in the marshes in the winter. The freshwater marshes in this part of North Carolina benefit from controlled burning to prevent the invasion of shrubby vegetation.

## Conservation Highlights

The Nature Conservancy has worked with the Wildlife Resources Commission to protect the Northwest River Game Land. In 1997, the North Carolina Chapter purchased 235 acres of marsh along the North Landing River. In 1998, Highland Properties donated 63 acres of the Nellie Bell Ponds natural area to the Conservancy. In 1999, the Conservancy acquired two tracts totaling 733 acres at Nellie Bell Ponds. The Conservancy also purchased two tracts comprising 207 acres at Tulls Creek, a tributary of the Northwest River. All Conservancy property has been transferred to the Wildlife Resources Commission.

The game land is part of a larger wetland complex that extends into Virginia, where the Virginia Chapter of The Nature Conservancy is working to protect land along the North Landing and Northwest Rivers.

## Trip Planner

This area has multiple uses, including hunting. Downloadable maps of the game land and hunting schedules are available on

Snow geese (Bill Lea)

the Wildlife Resources Commission web site.

The Northwest River Game Land is only accessible by boat and is thus an ideal place to explore by canoe or kayak. A portion of the game land is included in the N.C. Coastal Plain Paddle Trails Guide (see www.ncsu.edu/paddletrails). Paddlers can put in at the bridge crossing on NC 168 at Tull Creek/Cowell's Creek and paddle approximately 10 miles downstream and take out at Tulls Creek Marina on SR 1222. The marina may charge a fee. You can also paddle upstream on this slow-moving stream.

## Ownership/Access

N.C. Wildlife Resources Commission
1 (800) 662-7137
www.ncwildlife.org

# north river game land

**Camden & Currituck Counties**
**19,939 acres**

## Features

The North River wetlands complex is a large network of relatively pristine swamp forests and freshwater marshes encompassing over 30,000 acres. The North River Game Land contains Indiantown Creek Cypress Forest, a natural area with nearly 2,000 acres of relatively mature swamp forest and some areas of bottomland forest. The game land also contains about 90 acres of virgin bald cypress. While bald cypress is a common tree in North Carolina's Coastal Plain swamps, virgin stands are rare.

Other parts of the swamp are dominated by swamp tupelo, water tupelo, and pumpkin ash, with red maple in the understory. A slightly higher area supports a small remnant of the much rarer nonriverine wet hardwood forest community dominated by cherrybark oak, southern red oak, swamp chestnut oak, and water oak.

Containing no improved roads, the North River is an important wildlife corridor for large mammals like black bear and bobcat and provides extensive forested habitat for migratory songbirds like prothonotary and Swainson's warblers.

## Conservation Highlights

In 1997, The Nature Conservancy acquired 1,421 acres of Indiantown Creek Cypress Forest and transferred it to the N.C. Wildlife Resources Commission. In 1998, the Conservancy purchased 529 acres along the North River from the Canal Wood Corporation that include high-quality examples of Atlantic white cedar forest and tidal freshwater marsh and transferred the property to the Wildlife Resources Commission.

## Trip Planner

This area has multiple uses, including hunting. Downloadable maps of the game land and hunting schedules are available on the Wildlife Resources Commission web site.

Portions of this area are featured in the Albemarle Region Canoe Trail system. Northeast of Camden, take US 158 and then go south on SR 1148. A marked canoe trail begins at a double culvert on SR 1148 and continues downstream past a boat ramp at the Camden-Currituck County line on SR 1147. This trail follows the headwaters of Indiantown Creek through beautiful hardwood and cypress swamps. The creek is slow moving, so it is easy to paddle upstream back to the put-in, or you may continue downstream to the wider sections of the river.

North River (Fred Annand)

## Ownership/Access
N.C. Wildlife Resources Commission
1 (800) 662-7137
www.ncwildlife.org

# roanoke river

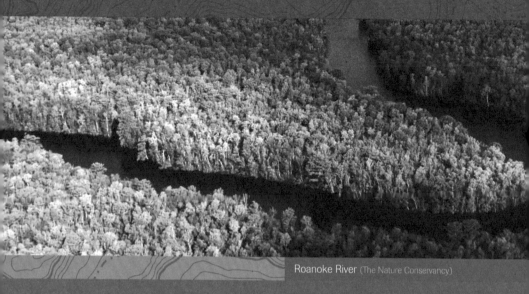

Roanoke River (The Nature Conservancy)

THE ROANOKE RIVER BEGINS AS A SWIFT MOUNTAIN STREAM IN THE BLUE RIDGE MOUNTAINS OF VIRGINIA. It journeys some 400 miles, slowing and broadening, before finally emptying into North Carolina's Albemarle Sound. The river stretches for 137 miles across North Carolina's Coastal Plain and its floodplain is up to five miles wide in some places. This floodplain contains the largest intact and least disturbed bottomland hardwood forest ecosystem remaining in the mid-Atlantic region. The middle section of the Roanoke River is characterized by alluvial forests and large back swamps, while the lower section contains vast tracts of bald cypress and water tupelo swamp forests. The Roanoke River provides a haven for a host of plants and animals, including more than 200 bird species.

Plant and animal species have adapted to thousands of years of flooding on the Roanoke River. Within the last half-century, the river has been shaped by three dams that sit near the Virginia/North Carolina border.

The dams curb major flooding on the river, while increasing the duration of minor deluges. Even water-loving cypress trees, which can live for hundreds of years, require a dry period for their seedlings to survive.

To help mend the problems created from this artificial flow, The Nature Conservancy has worked closely with both the U.S. Army Corps of Engineers and Dominion Generation, which owns and operates the dams. Conservation partners achieved a major success in 2005, when Dominion Generation agreed to ecological considerations that benefited the river and the species that depend on it. The partners continue to work together to attain healthy and productive ecosystems on the Roanoke.

The Nature Conservancy uses a philosophy called "adaptive management," in which scientific research determines the best way to solve a problem. For the Roanoke, models show that minor alterations to the existing system can mimic more natural flows of the river—to the great benefit of river species—

Roanoke paddle trail (The Nature Conservancy)

while generating only slightly less power. Adaptive management will continue to direct the policies of the Conservancy and its partners as future challenges arise.

The Nature Conservancy envisions that the Roanoke River will be managed so that conservation of natural resources and native ecosystems, recreation, flood control, economic development, and hydropower production are balanced in ecologically and economically sustainable ways.

# camassia slopes preserve

**Northampton County • 176 acres**

## Features

Wildflower enthusiasts will love taking a field trip to Camassia Slopes Preserve in the lower Roanoke River floodplain. Located on the north bank of the Roanoke River, Camassia Slopes has unusual soil types for the Coastal Plain, with highly basic soils more commonly found on midwestern river banks. The preserve is named for the wild hyacinth (*Camassia scilloides*) that grows abundantly in the area's hardwood forest and is rare east of the Appalachians. The preserve contains other wildflower species considered rare in North Carolina: sessile trillium, wild blue phlox, purple larkspur, and three-birds orchid. In all, more than two dozen species of endangered, uncommon, or rare wildflowers are found at Camassia Slopes.

This unusual assemblage of plant species is thought to be a remnant from the ice age some 220,000 to 400,000 years ago. The preserve's highly basic soil and terraced slopes, with angles of 15 to 35 degrees, enable these unique species to thrive here.

Large numbers of neotropical migratory birds can be seen throughout the Roanoke River floodplain in the spring and summer. Prothonotary warbler, Louisiana waterthrush, American redstart, and the rare cerulean warbler are some of the neotropical migratory songbirds that nest at Camassia Slopes. The preserve is also a good spot to see wild turkey.

## Conservation Highlights

In 1982, Union Camp Corporation donated Camassia Slopes to The Nature Conservancy and helped establish the Conservancy's first preserve in the lower Roanoke River floodplain. Invasive nonnative weeds are threatening Camassia Slopes, so Nature Conservancy staff and volunteers are working to combat invasive species such as Chinese privet, Japanese honeysuckle, and Japanese stilt grass.

## Trip Planner

This Nature Conservancy preserve is only accessible through the North Carolina Chapter field trip program. To find out about the program, contact the Roanoke River office for details.

## Ownership/Access

The Nature Conservancy
Roanoke River Office
P.O. Box 327
Halifax, NC 27839
(252) 583-0007
www.nature.org/northcarolina

Camassia Slopes woods (Jodie LaPoint)

# larkspur ridge preserve

**Halifax County • 97 acres**

## Features

Late March to early April is an ideal time to see the magnificent wildflower display in this preserve along the Roanoke River. Larkspur Ridge is home to at least two plants that are considered rare in North Carolina: sessile trillium and false rue anemone. Named after the locally rare purple larkspur, Larkspur Ridge is an unusually rich example of a moist hardwood forest. The ridge is part of an ancient floodplain terrace formed by sediments deposited by the Roanoke River. The nature preserve is now covered by a mature forest with patches of old-growth trees located on a series of steep, north-facing slopes that rise up to 75 feet above the river. Shagbark hickory and other hardwoods, some well over 100 years old, dominate the forest. The combination of north-facing slopes and alkaline soils has created an environment that is relatively cooler, moister, and richer in soil nutrients than the surrounding region. The area supports an abundance of wildlife such as river otter and woodchuck. Large numbers of neotropical migratory birds can be seen throughout the Roanoke River floodplain in the spring and summer.

## Conservation Highlights

The previous landowner, the Fenner family of Rocky Mount, registered this natural area with the N.C. Natural Heritage Program in 1982. The Nature Conservancy purchased 97 acres from the family in 1991.

## Trip Planner

This Nature Conservancy preserve is only accessible through the North Carolina Chapter's field trip program. To find out about the program, contact the Roanoke River office for details.

## Ownership/Access

The Nature Conservancy
Roanoke River Office
P.O. Box 327
Halifax, NC 27839
(252) 583-0007
www.nature.org/northcarolina

Larkspur (Mark Daniels)

# roanoke river wetlands game land

**Bertie, Halifax, Martin, Northampton, & Washington Counties • 26,506 acres**

## Features

The game land offers important wetland and bottomland-hardwood habitats. Several hundred species of birds have been documented in the area. The wetlands provide good winter habitat for a number of migratory birds, including waterfowl such as black duck, wood duck, and mallard. Wild turkey is also common in the area. It is also a valuable habitat for deer, fox, bobcat, squirrel, and the occasional black bear.

## Conservation Highlights

In 2006, The Nature Conservancy acquired nearly 220,000 acres of forestland across 10 states from International Paper Company. This was the single largest private land conservation sale in the history of the South, and one of the largest in the nation. As part of that deal, the Conservancy purchased 10,027 acres from International Paper, which were later transferred to the Wildlife Resources Commission for inclusion in the Roanoke River Wetlands Game Land.

## Trip Planner

This area has multiple uses, including hunting. Downloadable maps of the game land and hunting schedules are available on the Wildlife Resources Commission web site.

## Ownership/Access

N.C. Wildlife Resources Commission
1 (800) 662-7137
www.ncwildlife.org

Roanoke paddle trail (The Nature Conservancy)

Cypress knees (Mark Daniels)

# devil's gut preserve

**Martin County • 1,046 acres**

## Features

Located near the town of Jamesville in the lower Roanoke River floodplain, Devil's Gut Preserve consists of a relatively undisturbed old-growth bottomland hardwood and swamp forest. This area encompasses a broad diversity of landforms created by the migrating channel of the Roanoke River thousands of years ago. Long, narrow, sand or loamy ridges alternate with parallel bands of cypress-gum sloughs, forming a ridge-and-swale topography. Periodic flooding by the river and its companion, Devil's Gut, formed these features by depositing sediment. The low, flat ridges are probably ancient relics of natural levees, formed during floods when the river dumped huge amounts of sediment on its banks. The intermittently flooded cypress-gum sloughs probably occupy ancient filled river channels.

The preserve contains an old-growth water tupelo stand that is regarded as one of the best examples of this community type in North Carolina. Devil's Gut also contains several old-growth bald cypress trees that reach 130 feet in height and six feet in diameter. Devil's Gut is an important refuge for many species of wildlife including waterfowl, wild turkey, bobcat, river otter, and black bear. The area is known to support the rare Swainson's warbler and 54 other species of birds that use the area as breeding habitat. Devil's Gut is a wonderful destination for canoeing or kayaking.

## Conservation Highlights

In 1989, The Nature Conservancy purchased the property through a tax-free exchange from Mr. and Mrs. Charles P. Hayes.

## Trip Planner

This Nature Conservancy preserve is accessible through the North Carolina Chapter's field trip program. Contact the Roanoke River office for details.

## Ownership/Access

The Nature Conservancy
Roanoke River Office
P.O. Box 327
Halifax, NC 27839
(252) 583-0007
www.nature.org/northcarolina

Oak fungus (Jodie LaPoint)

**Beaufort & Washington Counties
5,482 acres**

## Features

Originally covering much of southwestern Washington County, Van Swamp once comprised nearly 13,500 acres extending from south of Plymouth into northern Beaufort County. Parallel north-south trending scarps border both the west and east margins of this swamp. These scarps are old beach ridges that formed when the Atlantic Ocean was much higher, during the Pleistocene Era.

One of the largest nonriverine swamp forest natural communities in the state, Van Swamp is dominated by swamp tupelo and contains one of the finest old-growth stands of this species known in North Carolina. The forest also contains large individual trees of several bay forest species, such as sweetbay and loblolly bay. Loblolly pine, Atlantic white cedar, and bald cypress also grow in the game land. A type of pocosin vegetation called a pond pine woodland dominates much of the southern portion of the swamp and contains large (60- to 90-foot-high) pond pines over a dense layer of tall shrubs and small trees.

This almost impenetrable and seasonally flooded natural area provides superb habitat for large populations of black bear and bobcat. Black bears are primarily nocturnal, but they can be seen any time of day or night. Over 30 species of neotropical migratory songbirds breed in Van Swamp, including blackthroated green warbler, worm-eating warbler, and Swainson's warbler. Birds such as the pileated woodpecker and red-shouldered hawk that require sizable tracts for breeding also thrive in Van Swamp.

## Conservation Highlights

Thanks to two grants totaling $2.514 million from the Natural Heritage Trust Fund and a $1.172 million grant from the Clean Water Management Trust Fund, The Nature Conservancy purchased 5,482 acres of Van Swamp from The Timber Company in 2000. The acquisition saved the natural area from imminent threats of timbering and conversion to pine plantations. The Conservancy transferred the land to the N.C. Wildlife Resources Commission for inclusion in the game lands program. The N.C. Division of Soil and Water Conservation helped develop a comprehensive plan to improve the water quality downstream from Van Swamp. The Wildlife Resources Commission plans to restore the pine plantations to native hardwood swamp.

## Trip Planner

This area has multiple uses, including hunting. Downloadable maps of the game land and hunting schedules are available on the Wildlife Resources Commission web site.

The game land is located south of Plymouth and west of NC 32 and contains a network of roads that provide access for people on foot or bike. You can enter the game land via the gated roads off NC 32 and Hollis Road.

Two fawns (Bill Lea)

## Ownership/Access

N.C. Wildlife Resources Commission
1 (800) 662-7137
www.ncwildlife.org

# pettigrew state park

## Tyrrell & Washington Counties
### 4,300 acres

Many years ago, Native Americans made dugout canoes from the large cypress trees – burning the cypress and scraping them until only the shells were left. It is believed that the Algonquin sank the dugouts in Lake Phelps to preserve them between hunting/fishing seasons. Archaeologists have unearthed several of the dugouts, and two can be seen at the park information center.

## Features

Pettigrew State Park includes two major water-based natural areas—Lake Phelps and the Scuppernong River Preserve.

Lake Phelps is North Carolina's second largest natural lake and is believed to be almost 40,000 years old. While other nearby water bodies are murky, Phelps is quite clear and shallow, with an average depth of four and a half feet. There are no tributaries to Lake Phelps; it is totally rain-fed. There is a lovely old-growth forest—one of the last remaining in eastern North Carolina—on the lake's northern shore. Some of the bald cypress trees in the area have a girth of 10 feet.

The Scuppernong is a blackwater river that flows through Tyrrell and Washington Counties into the Albemarle Sound. This free-flowing river is a great place to canoe, birdwatch, and fish. The river's broad floodplain is composed of diverse wetland forest communities, including extensive swamp forests of bald cypress, pond pine, sweetgum, sweet bay, and significant stands of rare Atlantic white cedar. Some of the cedars are quite large, with diameters up to three feet and heights of 100 feet. The river's floodplain provides an important wildlife corridor between Alligator River and the Pocosin Lakes National Wildlife Refuge. Black bear, bobcat, and river otter are common in this area, with the deep organic soils and thick forest providing an almost impenetrable protective barrier on the shoreline.

## Conservation Highlights

Since 1989, the North Carolina Chapter has protected 2,948 acres on the river through separate purchases and donations. The property was transferred to the N.C. Division of Parks and Recreation for inclusion in the Scuppernong River portion of the park.

## Trip Planner

Pettigrew State Park is located seven miles south of Creswell off US 64. From US 64, take exit 558 to Creswell. Turn left at Main Street and go two miles (the road becomes Spruill's Bridge Road). Turn right on Thirty Foot Canal Road and drive for five miles. Turn left on Lake Shore Road; the park office is on the right.

The N.C. Division of Parks and Recreation operates campgrounds at the park, as well as a couple of large picnic shelters.

The Scuppernong River is best explored by small boat on day trips, since much of the land along the river is privately owned. The Scuppernong is included in the Albemarle Region Canoe Trail system. There is a public boat landing south of the town of Creswell

River otter (Bill Lea)

on Main Street. The Visitor Center in Columbia offers canoe access and a 0.75 mile boardwalk through a bottomland swamp bordering the river.

At press time the N.C. Division of Parks and Recreation had signed a contract that will allow park visitors to make advance registration for campsites, shelters, and other facilities via a toll-free number and online. The system should be functional by summer 2009 and information will be posted on the park web site at www.ncparks.gov.

## Ownership/Access

N.C. Division of Parks and Recreation
2252 Lake Shore Road
Creswell, NC 27928
(252) 797-4475
pettigrew@ncmail.net
www.ncparks.gov

# currituck banks

## Features

Heading north from Duck, NC 12 follows Currituck Banks, a 22-mile stretch of barrier island separating Currituck Sound from the Atlantic Ocean. Currituck Banks consists of a medley of coastal natural communities, including beaches, dunes, interdunal ponds, maritime shrub thickets, estuarine bays and coves, and vast brackish and freshwater marshes. Biogeographically, this is a transition area, containing southern-ranging sea oats and northern American beach grass.

This area is also experiencing intensive development.

Currituck Sound and its surrounding wetlands are important feeding areas in the Atlantic flyway for migratory waterfowl. Large numbers of migrating land birds and raptors, including hawks and peregrine falcons, pass through the area during the fall. A number of waterfowl winter in the area, including diving and puddle ducks, snow geese, and tundra swans.

## Conservation Highlights

The North Carolina Chapter has been involved in an ongoing effort to protect Currituck Banks since the chapter was formed in 1977. Ownership is split between the N.C. Division of Coastal Management and the U.S. Fish and Wildlife Service.

## Trip Planner

Kayaking is a good way to view the area without disturbing the wildlife. There are several

**Currituck County • 6,875 acres**

boat ramps that offer good access to the area:

- On the mainland, a Wildlife Resources Commission boat ramp on Currituck Sound is located south of Coinjock. From Kitty Hawk, drive north on NC 158 for 20 miles to NC 3 (Poplar Branch Road). Turn right and drive 2.2 miles to the end of the road and the boat ramp at Poplar Branch landing.

- From the NCDOT ferry docks on Knotts Island, drive north on NC 615 approximately two miles to SR 1259 (Brumley Road), turn right and look for the parking area and boat launch approximately 120 yards before the end of the road.

- A boat ramp is located to the water tower on NC 12 in Duck.

- A public boat ramp is located in Corolla at the historical Whale Head Club, just north of the Currituck Lighthouse on NC 12.

Currituck Banks is located north of Duck on NC 12 and north of the road's terminus. There are no paved roads north of Corolla. You can walk to the beach from Corolla or drive in a four-wheel-drive vehicle.

## Ownership/Access

N.C. Division of Coastal Management
P.O. Box 549
Kitty Hawk, NC 27949
(252) 261-8891
www.nccoastalreserve.net

Currituck National Wildlife Refuge
c/o Mackay Island National Wildlife Refuge
P.O. Box 39
Knotts Island, NC 27950
(252) 429-3100
fws.gov/mackayisland/currituck

(John Warner)

# kitty hawk woods coastal reserve

**Dare County • 1,820 acres**

Kitty Hawk Woods is part of the N.C. Coastal Reserve System.

## Features

Located on the widest part of Currituck Banks, Kitty Hawk Woods is a maritime deciduous forest with low, gently rolling dune ridges interspersed with wet swales. These dune ridges run parallel to the shoreline. The protected portion of the woods consists of a relatively undisturbed maritime forest with southern red oak, water oak, willow oak, and beech trees.

The wetland swale areas contain maritime swamp forest communities with sweet gum, black gum, and the Outer Banks' largest stand of bald cypress. Relict beach ridges harbor maritime deciduous forest, dominated by a mixture of hardwoods and loblolly pines. Both of these forest communities are globally rare; Nags Head Woods is the only other extensive maritime deciduous forest.

Maritime forests are good birding spots during the breeding season and fall migration. Among the birds that nest at Kitty Hawk Woods are the locally uncommon Swainson's warbler and a host of more common species such as Acadian flycatcher, white-eyed vireo, gray catbird, and pileated woodpecker. Cottonmouths are abundant in the wet swales.

## Conservation Highlights

The Nature Conservancy acquired most of this property from the Resolution Trust Corporation in the early 1990s on behalf of the N.C. Division of Coastal Management.

## Trip Planner

This natural area is located in the town of Kitty Hawk and is open to the public during daylight hours. The reserve lies south of US 158. The forest is accessible via Woods Road. The best access is on the multiuse trail that parallels Woods Road. Public parking is located on the north end of Woods Road behind the playground. At the end of Birch Lane, off of Treasure Street, you will find a two-mile hiking trail that goes through maritime forest dominated by bald cypress. This trail goes through the 460+ acres owned by the town of Kitty Hawk.

A series of hiking trails can be accessed near the intersection of Amadas Road and Colleton Road. There are also two boat access areas in the reserve. High Bridge Creek passes through the reserve and is accessible by kayak, canoe, and small boat. You can access the creek from the parking lot of Kitty Hawk Kayaks on US 158. You can park there for free, but ask permission in the business. The launch site for the creek is located in the rear of the parking lot. You can paddle through the reserve and into Kitty Hawk Bay for an 8.5-mile roundtrip paddle. A public boat ramp is located on Bob Perry Road, which is off West Kitty Hawk Road.

Maritime forest (Marge Limbert)

## Ownership/Access

N.C. Division of Coastal Management
P.O. Box 549
Kitty Hawk, NC 27949
(252) 261-8891
www.nccoastalreserve.net

# nags head woods ecological preserve

## Dare County • 1,092 acres

## Location

This extensive ecological preserve on North Carolina's Outer Banks protects a remarkable range of unique habitats, including forested dunes, interdune ponds, marshes, and wetlands.

Two of the largest active sand dunes on the East Coast—Run Hill and Jockey's Ridge—run along the northern and southern borders of the preserve respectively. These huge ancient dunes constantly move and change shape as the prevailing northeasterly winds blow sand into the forest, marsh, and sound. Shielded from the ocean winds by the dune ridges, Nags Head Woods features a diversity of plant and animal life that is unusual to find on a barrier island. Towering oaks, hickories, and beech trees—some hundreds of years old—rise from the sand and create a canopy of trees more typical of the mountains of the eastern United States. Over 100 species of birds have been documented at Nags Head Woods. The preserve is an important nesting area for more than 50 species, including green heron, wood duck, red-shouldered hawk, clapper rail, ruby-throated hummingbird, pileated woodpecker, prothonotary warbler, and summer tanager. Fifteen species of amphibians and 28 species of reptiles have been documented as well. The freshwater ponds are inhabited by seven species of fish

and many reptiles and amphibians in addition to a great diversity of floating aquatic plant life, including the rare water violet. An extensive marsh system bordering Roanoke Sound on the western side of the preserve supports a wealth of wildlife including river otter, egrets, herons, and many species of migratory waterfowl.

During the 19th century and through the 1930s, Nags Head Woods was a thriving village community with 13 home sites, two churches, a school, a store, farms, a gristmill, and a shingle factory. There are artifacts remaining of village life: a home foundation, cemeteries, and other signs of previous human habitation in the forest.

## Conservation Highlights

Nags Head Woods was designated a National Natural Landmark in 1974, and protecting its unique habitats was one of the Conservancy's first priorities in North Carolina. Between 1978 and 1986, the Conservancy acquired about 420 acres in the northern section of the forest; some of the land was generously donated by John and Rhoda Calfee and Diane St. Clair. Partnerships with local municipalities were formed early in the process, with the leasing of 350 acres from the Town of Nags Head. In 1992, the Conservancy and the Town of Nags Head jointly acquired an additional 389 acres in the forest from Resolution Trust Corporation. In 1997, the Town of Nags Head agreed to dedicate nearly 300 acres of Nags Head Woods as a permanent conservation area under the State Nature Preserves Act. In addition, the Town of Kill Devil Hills signed a Memorandum of Understanding with The Nature Conservancy, placing another 100 acres in the forest under cooperative management. Working with the towns and other partners, The Nature Conservancy has succeeded in protecting this fragile ecosystem, overseeing both terrestrial and marine research and monitoring programs and providing trails for visitors to enjoy.

## Trip Planner

This preserve is open to the public from dawn until dusk every day of the week.

To visit the preserve take US 158 to Kill Devil Hills. Turn west near milepost 9 1/2 on Ocean Acres Drive and drive through a residential subdivision for a mile until you reach the entrance to Nags Head Woods Preserve. Trail maps and guides are available at the outdoor information counter.

Dogs are welcome on the preserve roads, but not on preserve trails.

Tree at Nags Head (Mark Daniels)

## Ownership/Access

The Nature·Conservancy
Nags Head Woods Ecological Preserve
701 West Ocean Acres Drive
Kill Devil Hills, NC 27948
(252) 441-2525
www.nature.org/northcarolina

# jockey's ridge state park

## Dare County • 420 acres

### Features

Jockey's Ridge is the tallest natural sand dune system in the eastern United States. The dunes vary from 80 feet to 120 feet high, depending on weather conditions.

Jockey's Ridge is an example of a medano—a huge, asymmetrical, shifting hill of sand lacking vegetation. Jockey's Ridge State Park is a small remnant of a dune system that once stretched for many miles along the coastline. This dune, together with the Run Hill dune, borders Nags Head Woods and shields the fragile maritime forest from wind shear and salt spray.

Unique plant and animal life has evolved in the harsh desert-like environment at Jockey's Ridge. The bare dune, maritime shrub thickets, and woods at the base of the dune are home to migratory birds, gray fox, racerunner lizards, and beetles.

### Conservation Highlights

The Nature Conservancy and the N.C. Division of Parks and Recreation began protecting Jockey's Ridge in 1974 as the Outer Banks became an increasingly popular vacation destination. Nags Head Woods, a Nature Conservancy preserve with a visitors' center and trail system, is a few miles north of the park and is included in this guide.

### Trip Planner

The park entrance is on the sound side of the town of Nags Head at milepost 12 on US 158 Bypass. Turn on Carolista Drive and follow the signs.

Paddlers (Charlie Peek)

(Charlie Peek)

## Ownership/Access

N.C. Division of Parks and Recreation
P.O. Box 592
Nags Head, NC 27959
(252) 441-7132
jockeys.ridge@ncmail.net
www.ncparks.gov

# buxton woods coastal reserve

**Dare County • 1,725 acres**

## Features

At 2,500 acres, Buxton Woods is the largest maritime forest remaining on North Carolina's barrier islands. Located on the cape of Hatteras Island near the town of Buxton, the forest has an extensive area of relict dunes stabilized by a maritime evergreen forest of mixed hardwoods and pines. The preserve also contains such unique natural communities as maritime swamp forest and maritime shrub swamp, open water interdune ponds, and unique marshy wetlands known as sedges.

The forest's great natural diversity can be attributed to the sheltering effects of the ancient dunes and the moderating temperatures on the cape. Over a dozen rare plant and animal species occur here, some at the northern end of their range. At least 135 species of birds have been recorded in the woods. Buxton Woods is an important resting area for migratory songbirds and raptors during fall migration. You may spot swallow-tailed kites here in May when they overshoot their South Carolina nesting sites.

## Conservation Highlights

In 1993 and 1994, The Nature Conservancy worked with the N.C. Division of Coastal Management to protect almost half of the forest. The natural area is now managed as part of the N.C. Coastal Reserve system.

## Trip Planner

The best way to enter the forest is to drive south of the Hatteras Island Visitor Center to the corner of NC 12 and Open Pond Road near the town of Buxton. Here you can hike on an interpretive loop trail that winds through the forest and goes by a marsh and a section of the Mountains-to-Sea Trail. Camping is available at a National Park Service campground at Cape Point near Buxton Woods.

## Ownership/Access

N.C. Division of Coastal Management
Northern Sites Manager
983 West Kitty Hawk Road
Kitty Hawk, NC 27949
(252) 261-8891
www.ncnerr.org

Marsh (Mark Daniels)

**Dare County • 1,766 acres**

## Features

As you drive through Manteo on your way to the northern Outer Banks, the US 64 bridge takes you over Roanoke Sound and the Roanoke Island Marshes. One of the largest undisturbed expanses of black needlerush marsh remaining in North Carolina, the Roanoke Island Marshes also contain loblolly pine and cedar-covered hummocks. The marshes provide important feeding habitat for river otter, wading birds, and shorebirds, including black duck, gadwall, and clapper rails. Tundra swans are also occasional visitors to the area.

Birders will be interested to know that the marshes support a breeding population of the state's significantly rare black rail. This secretive nocturnal rail is on the must-see lists of many birders and is a species of special concern due to its declining numbers and loss of habitat. Most birders who venture in the aptly named needlerush only hear the bird; it is very difficult to spot.

## Conservation Highlights

The Nature Conservancy helped protect this land through a combination of purchases and donations. Louis and Dora Midgette generously donated installment gifts of land to the Conservancy throughout the 1990s and the Conservancy transferred the marshland to the N.C. Wildlife Resources Commission.

## Trip Planner

You get a good view of the marshes as you head east on US 64 a couple of miles past Manteo. To access a parking area where you can view the marshes or put in a kayak, from the junction of US 64/264 and NC 345 east of Manteo, drive east on US 64/264 for one mile to Washington Baum Bridge. Turn right onto the access road at the bridge opposite Pirate's Cove Marina. The boat launch is under the west end of the bridge.

Kayakers should note that this launch is located on Roanoke Sound and can have a lot of boat traffic in the tourist season. Please bring maps and be informed about weather and wind conditions. You can paddle into the marsh by heading south from the launch for about a quarter-mile and then turning right in John's Ditch, which leads to Sand Beach Creek and eventually empties into Broad Creek.

This area has multiple uses, including hunting. Downloadable maps of the game land and hunting schedules are available on the Wildlife Resources Commission web site..

## Ownership/Access

N.C. Wildlife Resources Commission
1 (800) 662-7137
www.ncwildlife.org

(John Warner)

**Dare & Hyde Counties • 258,000 acres**

## Features

Primarily a tangle of low pocosin and nonriverine swamp forest, this area contains almost all of the wetland habitats associated with peatlands. Pocosin means "swamp on a hill," an apt description of these dense evergreen shrub bogs that develop over deep wet layers of peat. The swamp forests are characterized by loblolly pine, pond pine, and white cedar.

Alligator River is home to a number of neotropical migratory birds including the prothonotary warbler, prairie warbler, black-throated green warbler, and Swainson's warbler. It also provides valuable habitat for black bear, bobcat, river otter, and the red wolf, and is the northernmost range for the American alligator.

Containing over 1,000 miles of estuarine shoreline, as well as many miles of slow-moving blackwater streams, this wild area offers a great place to hone your paddling skills. Alligator River, Milltail Creek, Sawyer Lake, and the connecting creeks and canals comprise an excellent canoe trail system that provides the easiest access to this expansive refuge.

In 1987 the U.S. Fish and Wildlife Service released captive-bred red wolves in the refuge. Once common in the Southeast, this species became extinct in the wild because of hunting and loss of habitat. The red wolf population in the area is now recovering, with between 100 and 130 free-ranging wolves. The red wolf is an elusive nocturnal animal, so you probably will not see it on your visit to the refuge. But check with the refuge office to learn about their wolf howling excursions, which provide opportunities to hear the wolves' unforgettable call as they roam through the swamp forests.

Be warned that ravenous deer flies emerge in the hotter months. Spring is a good time to go birding, and fall and winter are pleasant times to visit, when temperatures are more moderate.

## Conservation Highlights

The Nature Conservancy has protected 190,013 acres in the Alligator River area—all have been transferred to the state or federal government. First Colony Farms once owned this area, but its efforts to convert the land for agriculture and peat mining proved too costly. From 1980 to 1984 The Nature Conservancy helped create the Alligator River National Wildlife Refuge by arranging a gift from Prudential Insurance Company of 118,000 acres and purchasing 25,000 acres of adjacent land. At the time, the Prudential donation was valued at more than $50 million and was the largest conservation gift in history.

In a milestone effort in 2007, The Nature Conservancy acquired 3,376 acres along the Alligator River on behalf of the state, and the Wildlife Resources Commission acquired another 5,101 acres. These parcels represent the last remaining large tracts along the Alligator River shoreline. With their conservation, the entire shoreline—approximately 75 miles—of the Alligator River is permanently protected.

## Trip Planner

If you plan to drive into the refuge, we advise you to use a four-wheel-drive vehicle, since rain can turn the roads to mud. US 264 traverses the refuge's southern and eastern sections and offers good views of wetland habitats. US 64 passes through the northern sector, where unpaved side roads lead into the refuge. There is an information kiosk, a handicapped-accessible half-mile trail, and a paved parking lot at the Milltail Road entrance, 4.4 miles west of the US 64/264 intersection. The Buffalo City Road runs south from US 64 to a boat ramp on Milltail Creek 4.2 miles east of the Alligator River (7.7 miles west of the 64/264 junction).

There is a canoe/kayak trail at this point that is part of the Albemarle Region Canoe Trail system. Other paddling trails can be found off NC 94 at the bridge just south of Gum Neck. You can either paddle upstream on the northwest or southwest fork or head downstream to more open water. We recommend these areas for day trips only, as there is very little high ground for getting out of your boat and stretching your legs.

Hunting is allowed on the Gull Rock Game Land and the Alligator River National Wildlife Refuge. Downloadable maps of the game land and hunting schedules are available on the Wildlife Resources Commission web site, www.ncwildlife.org. Information about hunting at the refuge is available at www.fws.gov/refuges.

(Debbie Crane)

## Ownership/Access

There are three large owners of public property on the Alligator—the U.S. Fish and Wildlife Service, the N.C. Wildlife Resources Commission, and the N.C. Division of Coastal Management.

Alligator River National Wildlife Refuge
P.O. Box 1969
Manteo, NC 27954
(252) 473-1131
alligatorriver@fws.gov

Gull Rock Game Land
N.C. Wildlife Resources Commission
1 (800) 662-7137
www.ncwildlife.org

Emily and Richardson Preyer Buckridge Preserve
N.C. Division of Coastal Management
P.O. Box 8
Columbia, NC 27925
(252) 796-3709
www.nccoastalreserve.net

**Hyde County • 16,411 acres**

## Features

Swanquarter National Wildlife Refuge is composed of islands and coastal marshlands containing potholes, creeks, swamp forests and tidal drains. This brackish marsh ecosystem is dominated by black needlerush and other marsh grasses. Tens of thousands of canvasback, bufflehead, redhead, and ruddy ducks winter in adjacent bays and are visible from the Swan Quarter–Ocracoke ferry as it leaves Swan Quarter and passes by refuge waters. Many bird species nest here, including egrets, osprey, and other raptors. The refuge contains a stand of old-growth bald cypress that supports a great blue heron rookery. This protected land is an important corridor between Pamlico Sound and Lake Mattamuskeet National Wildlife Refuge.

## Conservation Highlights

In 1980, The Nature Conservancy acquired 140 acres of wetlands, which was transferred to the refuge. Another 758 acres were donated by Transamerica Insurance Company to The Nature Conservancy in 1991 and transferred to the refuge.

## Trip Planner

The refuge is located south of Belhaven, North Carolina, and southwest of Lake Mattamuskeet, on the south side of US 264 on the Rose Bay access road marked from US 264. The state ferry landing and private boat ramp are located south of the town of Swan Quarter via NC 45 and SR 1132. To get to the fishing pier and canoe or kayak put-in from Swan Quarter, drive six miles west on US 264, turn left on a gravel access road, and go two miles to the parking area and pier.

Hunting is also allowed at national wildlife refuges. You can check on refuge hunting schedules on www.fws.gov/refuges.

## Ownership/Access

U.S. Fish and Wildlife Service
Swanquarter National Wildlife Refuge
2 Mattamuskeet Road
Swanquarter, NC 27885
(252) 926-4021
www.fws.gov/refuges

Tundra swans on Lake Mattamuskeet (Jodie LaPoint)

Long leaf pine and wiregrass (Jodie LaPoint)

THE SANDHILLS REGION OCCUPIES A LARGE AREA OF SOUTHEASTERN NORTH CAROLINA, AND IS STILL CHARACTERIZED BY EXTENSIVE CANOPIES OF LONGLEAF PINE FORESTS SUPPORTING SOME OF THE RICHEST NATURAL COMMUNITIES IN NORTH CAROLINA. Once spreading from Virginia to Texas, longleaf pine forests today cover only about three to five percent of their original range.

The Sandhills is home to many threatened plants and animals, but perhaps the best-known is the red-cockaded woodpecker.

The Sandhills hosts the second-largest remaining population of this federally endangered bird. In 2005, the Conservancy and its partners celebrated the first-ever recovery of the red-cockaded woodpecker—five years earlier than projected.

Threats to this ecosystem include fire suppression—which the longleaf pine communities need to maintain their natural equilibrium—and detrimental forestry practices, development, and intensive land uses such as pine plantations.

Wiregrass regrowing after a burn (The Nature Conservancy)

**Moore, Richmond, & Scotland Counties**
**58,713 acres**

## Features

The Sandhills Game Land comprises one of the most extensive and accessible longleaf pine habitats in North Carolina. Offering a great cross-section of the topography and habitat typical of the Sandhills region, the game land contains longleaf pine woodlands, streamhead pocosins, and seepage bogs. The area's rolling topography distinguishes it from the flatter and lower terrain of the outer Coastal Plain. The N.C. Wildlife Resources Commission manages the area with controlled burns, which help maintain the various longleaf pine communities.

One of the most interesting areas within the game land is Horse Creek Longleaf Forest. Located near Pinebluff, the Horse Creek Forest provides an important corridor between two major red-cockaded woodpecker populations in the Sandhills Game Land/ Camp Mackall and Southern Pines/Pinehurst/ Fort Bragg areas. This forest is a peaceful spot distinguished by old-growth longleaf pines estimated to be more than 100 years old, which tower over a healthy wiregrass ground cover. Wild turkey, quail, and fox squirrel also inhabit the property. If you visit Horse Creek you might spot the remains of a fox squirrel snack—this large squirrel shreds the massive longleaf pine cones to extract the tasty seeds.

The Wildlife Resources Commission is working to attract nesting pairs of the federally endangered red-cockaded woodpecker to the site by building artificial nesting cavities. The woodpeckers inhabit mature pine forest that typically contained longleaf pines averaging 80 to 120 years old and/or loblolly pines averaging 70 to 100 years. This is the only woodpecker that excavates nesting cavities in living trees. Red-cockaded woodpeckers need from one to several years to create a suitable nesting cavity, which is much longer than other woodpecker species that use dead trees and snags for nesting cavities.

## Conservation Highlights

Over the years, the Conservancy has protected 3,896 acres in the area that have been transferred to the Wildlife Resources Commission. At press time, three recent purchases, all in Scotland County in 2008, had not yet been transferred to the Wildlife Resources Commission, including the 102-acre Wilkes tract on Drowning Creek, the 16-acre Bennie tract on NC 15-501, and the 247-acre Smith tract also on NC 15-501.

## Trip Planner

This area is open to the public for multiple uses, including hunting. Downloadable maps of the game land and hunting schedules are available on the Wildlife Resources Commission web site.

The Department of Defense also uses the game land for training exercises, so visitors may encounter military personnel. An extensive system of dirt and sand roads crisscrosses the property; drivers and bikers should be aware that there is deep sand in some areas.

One popular site in the game land is Scotland Lane. The Wildlife Resources Commission burns this 30-acre site every year, so the longleaf forest here is thriving. During the growing season, be sure to look for the pitcher plants and orchids that grow in the low-lying seeps in the area. To reach Scotland Lane from the town of Hoffman, from the intersection of US 1/SR 1475, drive south for two miles on US 1. Turn left on Old Lauren Hill Road (SR 1346), cross the railroad tracks, and drive approximately 1.5 miles. (At this point you will be on dirt roads.) At the first main graded intersection, turn left on the unmarked dirt road and drive approximately 0.5 mile and park. Scotland Lane is on the right side of the road.

A second popular site is Horse Creek. From the town of Pinebluff, drive south on US 1 for about two miles to the intersection with Thunder Road/Addor Road (SR 1102). Turn right on Thunder Road, and right after you pass the water treatment plant, turn right on an unmarked, semimaintained gravel road. Drive approximately 0.75 mile. The road intersects with the game land boundary, so look for game land signs. If you take a right here, there are access trails into Horse Creek on the left side of the road.

Controlled burn (The Nature Conservancy)

## Ownership/Access

N.C. Wildlife Resources Commission
1 (800) 662-7137
www.ncwildlife.org

**Moore County • 898 acres**

## Features

This longleaf ecosystem is open and grassy, with gentle rolling hills and longleaf pines spread across the landscape. It contains a variety of Sandhills habitats: upland sand ridges, where turkey oaks tower over wiregrass; branch heads and stream tributaries, with their bottomland hardwoods and bay vegetation; and a small grass-sedge bog. The Boyd Estate tract is especially significant because it harbors a virgin stand of longleaf pine bounded by mature black oaks. The pines in this tract are over 200 years old.

Rare or uncommon species at Weymouth Woods include the red-cockaded woodpecker, eastern fox squirrel, pine barrens tree frog, and bog spicebush. Commonly seen wildlife includes salamanders, snakes, skinks, and box turtles. The park staff conducts controlled burns to mimic the natural fires that many plants in the Sandhills region need to survive.

Paint Hill is a satellite of Weymouth Woods Preserve, distinguished by a rugged topography, with slopes reaching 618 feet. The name refers to the reddish clay hardpan soil that impedes the downward percolation of water, creating a habitat favored by wetland species on the upland slopes. Paint Hill has a canopy of longleaf pine, some scrub oaks, and a ground cover that includes a mix of wiregrass, creeping blueberry, and the rare Sandhills pyxie-moss, which is essentially restricted to the Sandhills region of the state.

## Conservation Highlights

In 1963 the Conservancy and the N.C. Division of Parks and Recreation sought to preserve Weymouth Woods by working with Katharine Boyd to protect her estate and establish North Carolina's first natural area in the state park system. More land was added to Weymouth Woods in 1979 with the help of Friends of Weymouth, Inc. Thanks to a series of bargain sales from the Ives family, the N.C. Division of Parks and Recreation and The Nature Conservancy are working to protect the entire Paint Hill natural area.

## Trip Planner

The preserve is open to hikers year-round. Head one mile southeast from Southern Pines on US 1, turn east onto Saunders Boulevard (SR 2053), go 1.3 miles, and turn left onto Bethesda Road (SR 2074). This road becomes Fort Bragg Road, and the preserve entrance is located a few miles down the road on the left.

## Ownership/Access

North Carolina Division of Parks and Recreation
Weymouth Woods Sandhills Nature Preserve
1024 N. Fort Bragg Road
Southern Pines, NC 28387
(910) 692-2167
weymouth.woods@ncmail.net
www.ncparks.gov

Pine with woodpecker nest (Ryan Elting)

**Cumberland County • 2,829 acres**

## Features

One of the most endangered ecosystems in the country, the remaining longleaf habitat is threatened by development, fire suppression, and conversion to loblolly pine plantations.

Longleaf pine savannas can support as many as 50 different plant species in one square meter. Fire is woven into the life cycles of many plants and animals: longleaf seedlings can only germinate in an open, fire-maintained understory, while red-cockaded woodpeckers nest almost exclusively in mature stands of fire-dependent longleaf.

## Conservation Highlights

In 2001, The Nature Conservancy purchased the 1,173-acre Carvers Creek Preserve in Cumberland County, just north of Fayetteville on the eastern edge of the Sandhills. The preserve protects a mosaic of Sandhills communities, including pine–scrub oak sandhill, and wetland areas such as seeps, stream pocosins, and a small swamp. The natural area is home to several active red-cockaded woodpecker colonies and several populations of Sandhills pyxie-moss. The 222-acre Wood tract was added to Carvers Creek just before the property was transferred to State Parks in 2006.

In 2009 The Nature Conservancy's Long Valley Farm, a historic 1,435-acre estate straddling the Cumberland and Harnett county line, will be donated to the state as an addition to Carvers Creek State Park.

The Nature Conservancy is a member of the North Carolina Sandhills Conservation Partnership, a group of local, state, and federal partners working to conserve, protect and enhance the unique ecology of the Sandhills.

## Trip Planner

The North Carolina Division of Parks and Recreation is creating this state park. At press time, there are no facilities or public access at the site. Contact the N.C. Division of Parks and Recreation for a status update.

Red-cockaded woodpecker (John Ennis)

Carvers Creek swamp (Ida Phillips)

## Ownership/Access

1615 MSC
Raleigh, NC 27699
(919) 733-4181
www.ncparks.gov

## Hoke County • 3,288 acres

## Features

Longleaf pine forests once stretched 90 million acres from Virginia to Texas. Harvested for lumber, turpentine, tar, and pitch, this vast forest began to decline rapidly in the 19th century, and today only three to five percent of the original range remains. You can see what these ancient woodlands once looked like by visiting Calloway Forest, a longleaf pine forest in the Sandhills.

Plants found in longleaf pine forests include wiregrass, Michaux's sumac and rough-leaf loosestrife. The animals of the forest include woodpecker, migratory songbird, fox squirrel, and bobcat. Preserving forests like Calloway will help "bridge the gap" between existing protected areas by providing corridors for wildlife to migrate and also to make their home.

Many of these species depend on the openness of longleaf pine forest to forage and raise young. Due to fire suppression efforts in the late 20th century, much of the open longleaf pine forest became overgrown with hardwoods such as scrub oak, which have hampered the growth of other plants and trees and caused a decline in bobwhite quail and red-cockaded woodpecker.

The Conservancy, with the assistance of its conservation partners, has reintroduced fire into this landscape through controlled burns that reduce hardwoods and encourage the growth of fire-dependent species such as wiregrass and longleaf pine. Before the forest was acquired by the Conservancy, it was aggressively harvested for pine needles. So, in addition to fire, other important management techniques for the restoration of the forest include the collection and sowing of wiregrass seed and planting of longleaf seedlings.

## Conservation Highlights

Calloway Forest was protected through a collaborative effort between the Conservancy and state and federal agencies. The N.C. Department of Transportation purchased the tract as mitigation for effects on red-cockaded woodpecker habitat, established an endowment for its stewardship and then transferred it to the Conservancy. We are managing the forest in consultation with the U.S. Fish and Wildlife Service, and the preserve will eventually be included in the state's game lands program.

## Trip Planner

The preserve is open to visitors year round.

Visitors are welcome to explore the entire forest, but be aware that hunting is allowed during the season. A picnic area is available.

From Fayetteville or Raeford, take US 211 West. Look for Calloway Road on the left. The park is on the right, a tenth of a mile past Calloway Road. From Aberdeen, take US 211 East. The park entrance is on the left, three miles past the B.P. gas station.

Longleaf seedling after burn (Marge Limbert)

## Ownership/Access

The Nature Conservancy
Sandhills Project Office
P.O. Box 206
140 SW Broad Street
Southern Pines, NC 28388
(910) 246-0300
www.nature.org/northcarolina

# long valley farm

**Cumberland & Harnett Counties**
**1,435 acres**

## Features

When biologists from the Conservancy and the North Carolina Natural Heritage Program inventoried this property in 2002, they found a number of interesting natural areas, from healthy stands of longleaf pine to a cypress-gum swamp with canopy trees 100 feet tall and wet meadows that support a number of carnivorous plant species such as pitcher plants and sundews. Long Valley Farm supports rare bird species as well: Bachman's sparrow and the loggerhead shrike have been observed on the property, as has the federally listed red-cockaded woodpecker. The eastern fox squirrel is also present.

Long Valley Farm adds important habitat to augment The Nature Conservancy's landscape conservation plans in the Sandhills region. The Conservancy works to conserve longleaf pine habitat in the Sandhills, bridging the gap between already protected lands at Fort Bragg, Camp Mackall, and the Sandhills Game Land.

## Conservation Highlights

James Stillman Rockefeller, the longtime owner of Long Valley Farm, passed away in 2004 at age 102. He greatly desired to see the farm permanently protected from development and bequeathed the property to The Nature Conservancy in his will. In the 1920s, Long Valley Farm was originally established as part of the Overhills estate by

Rockefeller's uncle Percy. It is listed in the National Register of Historic Places.

Approximately two-thirds of Long Valley Farm's 1,380 acres are wooded, with the remainder consisting of pasture and farm fields and a number of structures, including a large home used by Rockefeller. Over the many years the property belonged to the Rockefeller family, it produced everything from cattle and tobacco to timber and turpentine.

The Nature Conservancy has restored several hundred acres of fields to longleaf pine and/or native warm-season grasses. In addition, the N.C. Ecosystem Enhancement Program (EEP) is restoring over two miles of stream channel and adjacent wetlands. When opened to the public, Long Valley Farm will be a wonderful example of the longleaf pine forest restoration efforts that are beginning to take hold across the Southeast.

## Trip Planner

Long Valley Farm is owned by The Nature Conservancy, which is developing a management plan for the property. The property will not be open to the public during the Conservancy's planning phase, but it is expected that the property will open in the near future, probably as a part of the state park system. To find out its current status, contact The Nature Conservancy at (919) 403-8558.

(The Nature Conservancy)

## Ownership/Access

The Nature Conservancy
4705 University Drive, Suite 290
Durham, NC 27707
(919) 403-8558
www.nature.org/northcarolina

## Features

Slogging through the shallow water of a flooded Carolina bay is not for the faint at heart. The bottom is slippery and the critters are slimy. But once you get used to the environment, a trip to the Carolina bays can be a great lesson in wetland ecosystems.

People still debate the origin of these elliptical, seasonally flooded depressions, espousing theories ranging from meteor showers to extraterrestrial visitors. The most accepted theory is that wind and water activity during the last ice age formed the bays. Although over 400,000 Carolina bays dot the eastern seaboard from southern New Jersey to northern Florida, these land formations were not widely recognized until the advent of aerial photography in the 1930s, when photos revealed a bird's-eye view of the bays. The wetlands are called Carolina bays because most of them are found in the Carolinas and they tend to be dominated by three species of bay tree: Virginia bay, loblolly bay, and red bay.

Nearly all Carolina bays are situated on a northwest-southeast axis and have a high, sandy rim on the southeastern edge that often supports vegetation adapted to dry conditions, such as pine trees. Bays range in size from a fraction of an acre to over 5,000 acres. They are defined as either water-filled (bay lakes like Lake Waccamaw, which is described in this guide), peat-based, or clay-based.

Clay-based bays are the most threatened because they are easily converted to agricultural land. The clay-based bays' unique natural features vary, depending on seasonal water levels.

The Carolina Bay Preserves consist of eight separate Carolina Bays ranging in size from the 197-acre Antioch Church Bay to the 31-acre Hamby's Bay, both in Hoke County. Other bays included in the preserve are Dunahoe Bay (Robeson County), Goose Pond Bay (Robeson County), McIntosh Bay Complex (Scotland County), Oak Savannah Bay (Robeson County), Pretty Pond Bay (Robeson County), and State Line Prairie Bay (Scotland County, N.C./Marlboro County, S.C.).

The bays are ideal for reptiles and amphibians. At least 50 reptile and amphibian species live in North Carolina's bays, including rare species such as the tiger salamander and gopher frog. Most of their

breeding activity takes place in winter and spring when the bays are wet—they are usually dry by early summer.

Pond cypress, a smaller relative of bald cypress, is abundant in three of the Conservancy's bays. The cypress rise from the black shallow water, along with a brightly colored herbaceous display of yellow polygala, pink marsh fleabane, and sarvis holly, which has showy red berries in the fall. Dunahoe Bay is a prime nesting spot for hundreds of colonial water birds, species such as egrets and herons that nest in large colonies. Large numbers of cattle, great, and snowy egrets; anhingas; and little blue herons have nested in rookeries at the preserve in recent years. Inland rookeries such as Dunahoe Bay have become increasingly rare in North Carolina because of habitat loss and human disturbance.

### Conservation Highlights

The Conservancy has focused its efforts on endangered clay bays, working for a number of years with many different landowners to protect eight different clay-based Carolina bay preserves through purchases and donations.

### Trip Planner

Because of the fragile nature of the bays, they are only accessible through special arrangements with The Nature Conservancy. Visitors wanting to see Carolina Bays in person should consider visiting Lake Waccamaw State Park, which is the largest bay in the state, or Horseshoe Lake Game Land. Both are detailed elsewhere in this guide and are open to the public.

from left: Little blue heron (Bill Lea); Egret (Bill Lea)

### Ownership/Access

The Nature Conservancy
Sandhills Project Office
P.O. Box 206
Southern Pines, NC 28388
(910) 246-0300
www.nature.org/northcarolina

# lumber river state park

**Columbus, Hoke, Robeson, & Scotland Counties • 7,936 acres**

Recreation to acquire 2,632 acres for Lumber River State Park.

## Features

From its headwaters at the confluence of Drowning Creek and Buffalo Creek in Scotland County, the Lumber River flows freely for 115 miles through the Sandhills region of North Carolina and crosses into South Carolina, where it joins the Little Pee Dee River.

This National Wild and Scenic River and its floodplain contain many high-quality natural communities, including cypress-gum swamp and levee forest, as well as unusual upland communities, such as longleaf pine ridges. The extensive swamp forests along the Lumber River provide excellent habitat for river otter, waterfowl, and migratory songbirds. The river itself is home to American alligator and several species of fish, including the Cape Fear chub.

## Conservation Highlights

In 1989, the State of North Carolina designated the Lumber a State Natural and Scenic River. In 1998, the U.S. Department of the Interior designated 81 miles of the Lumber River as a state and locally managed component of the National Wild and Scenic River system. The Lumber is the fourth river in North Carolina to receive this national designation and the only blackwater river with this status. The Nature Conservancy has worked with the Lumber River Conservancy and the N.C. Division of Parks and

## Trip Planner

Lumber River State Park is best visited by canoe or small boat. The river holds many twists and turns and has lots of feeder streams to explore. Be sure to bring some maps along with your canoe and check with the park office for current river conditions.

The park office is located 12 miles east of Fairmont off NC 130 to SR 2225 on SR 2246. There are numerous road crossings and access points to the river. If you are interested in canoeing from the head of the river, Turnpike Road (SR 1412) crosses the river in Scotland County. There is also a Wildlife Resources Commission landing at the NC 72 crossing south of Lumberton, and bridges on US 74 or NC 904 farther downstream. The state park has a landing at Princess Ann, between the US 74 and NC 904 bridges. Follow SR 2225 south of Orrum to SR 2246 to reach the landing.

## Ownership/Access

N.C. Division of Parks and Recreation
Lumber River State Park
2819 Princess Ann Road
Orrum, NC 28369
(910) 628-4564
lumber.river@ncmail.net
www.ncparks.gov

Anhinga (Bill Lea)

**Bladen County • 47 acres**

## Features

The Cedar Swamp Seep Preserve is located in the Bladen Lakes region in northwestern Bladen County. This area is known for its many Carolina bays, a curious geomorphic feature. There are many theories as to how Carolina bays are formed, some citing meteors and others, glacial activity. The Cedar Swamp Seep Preserve sits on the northeast edge of Cedar Swamp Bay, which is one of the Carolina bays.

The Cedar Swamp Seep tract is dominated by Atlantic white cedar swamp that is kept moist by seepage from the hillside above. The western portion of the site is pine flatwoods, which transition into a narrow strip of xeric sandhill scrub to the east. The preserve is dominated by second- and third-growth Atlantic white cedar trees interspersed with a few red maple and black gum trees. The shrub layer includes laurel greenbrier, titi, and sweet pepperbush. The most common plants in the herbaceous layer include various sedges, sundew, and cinnamon fern; a continuous carpet of sphagnum moss is present where there is adequate light.

## Conservation Highlights

The Nature Conservancy's interest in the Cedar Swamp Seep was due to its high ecological value, particularly the presence of the Atlantic white cedar swamp. The site was acquired by The Nature Conservancy in 1987. The preserve was designated a North Carolina Natural Heritage Area in 1989.

## Trip Planner

The Cedar Swamp Seep Preserve is only accessible through the North Carolina Chapter's field trip program. Contact the North Carolina Chapter at (919) 403-8558 for details.

## Ownership/Access

North Carolina Chapter Office
The Nature Conservancy
4705 University Drive, Suite 290
Durham, NC 27707
(919) 403-8558
www.nature.org/northcarolina

Sundew (Marge Limbert)

# black river

Black River (Fred Annand)

THE BLACK RIVER, NOT SURPRISINGLY, IS A BLACKWATER RIVER. As tannins from decaying vegetation leach into the water, the river is stained its characteristic dark tea color.

The river is characterized by meanders, oxbows, artesian springs, and mature swamp forests.

The Black River and approximately 70 miles of two of its major tributaries are designated Outstanding Resource Waters by the N.C. Division of Water Quality. The relatively undisturbed Black River system has extraordinarily high water quality.

Tall, flat-topped bald cypress with huge buttresses completely dominate the sometimes open canopy in the old-growth stands. This extensive forest, including several trees ranging from 780 to 1,700 years in age, is considered to be the oldest stand of trees east of the Rocky Mountains.

Black River (Jodie LaPoint)

**Sampson County • 2,103 acres**

## Features

This preserve gets its name from the pondberry, which is one of the two most endangered plant species in North Carolina. Pondberry, also known as southern spicebush, was once found across the South in specialized wetland habitats. Pondberry is fire-dependent, meaning it needs regular fire to keep its habitat healthy. Suppressing fires has substantially reduced pondberry habitat—to the point where there are only two remaining populations in North Carolina. The low shrub with its lemony-fragrant foliage produces yellow flowers in late February and early March and red berries in the fall. The pondberries are found in one of the preserve's small clay-based Carolina bays.

The preserve's sandy uplands contain about 350 acres of mature longleaf pine. Biologists have found red-cockaded woodpecker nesting or cavity trees in the preserve's longleaf pine stand, although no active colonies of the bird have been documented. Rare Atlantic white cedar, also known as juniper, is also found in the preserve in seepage areas. Atlantic white cedar once ranged from Maine to South Carolina. It was the perfect tree from a timbering perspective—lightweight, resistant to rot and easy to turn—which led to heavy timbering.

## Conservation Highlights

In 2001, The Nature Conservancy purchased Pondberry Bay from Canal Forest Industries and in 2002 transferred the property to the N.C. Department of Agriculture's Plant Protection Section. Grants from the Natural Heritage Trust Fund and Clean Water Management Trust Fund helped fund the acquisition.

The Plant Conservation Program is working to restore the area, which includes conducting controlled burns to benefit fire-dependent species like pondberry and Atlantic white cedar.

## Trip Planner

Because of the rarity of the plant species on the preserve, access is by permit only. Inquiries should be made to the Department of Agriculture's Plant Protection Section.

## Ownership/Access

N.C. Department of Agriculture
Plant Protection Section
1060 Mail Service Center
Raleigh, NC 27699-1060
(919) 733-6930, ext. 231
www.ncagr.gov/plantindustry/plant/plantconserve/index.htm

Southern spicebush (Will Cook)

**Bladen, Cumberland, & Sampson Counties • 1,098 acres**

## Features

The South River is one of the most scenic rivers in North Carolina's Coastal Plain, offering a tranquil destination for boaters and anglers. Bald cypress draped in Spanish moss line the banks of the river as it winds its way through Cumberland, Bladen, and Sampson counties.

With a drainage area of approximately 500 square miles, the South River is the largest tributary of the Black River in the Cape Fear River basin. The river originates in Harnett County, where it is called the (Little) Black River. Just south of Dunn, near Mingo Swamp, the waterway becomes the South River. It flows along the western border of Sampson County, forming the eastern boundary of Cumberland and Bladen Counties, and joins the Black River near the Pender County line.

Most of the floodplain is heavily forested and lacks any industry, adding to the river's pristine nature. The State of North Carolina designated a portion of the river an Outstanding Resource Water in 1994 in recognition of its exceptional water quality and great diversity of aquatic species.

The higher portions of the river floodplain contain bottomland hardwood forest with various species of oaks, red maple, and rare Atlantic white cedar. Cypress-gum swamp, easily distinguished by its canopy of swamp tupelo, bald cypress, and pond cypress, is found in low-lying sloughs, swales, and backswamps.

Mammals such as black bear and bobcat inhabit the floodplain, while river otter and mink are often seen gamboling in the river and along its banks. Biologists have recorded several sightings of the rare Rafinesque's big-eared bat in cypress-gum swamps along the lower sections of the river. Considered a species of "special concern" in North Carolina, this bat roosts under bridges and in buildings and hollow trees in mature forests. Forest rivers like the South also provide an important habitat for neotropical migratory songbirds such as the prothonotary warbler.

Renowned for its excellent fish, the river boasts populations of largemouth bass, chain and redfin pickerel, and redbreast sunfish. Biologists have also discovered two rare fish species in the river that are endemic to the Carolinas—the Santee chub and the broadtail madtom.

## Conservation Highlights

In recent years, The Nature Conservancy and the N.C. Coastal Land Trust have worked to protect this river using a $2.5 million grant from the N.C. Clean Water Management Trust Fund. In 2000, the Nature Conservancy purchased its first property, the 306-acre Daughtry tract, along the river from The Timber Company. That same year, the Henry Rankin family donated 40 acres in Cumberland County to The Nature Conservancy. The N.C. Coastal Land Trust has protected an additional 711 acres along the river.

(Bill Lea)

## Trip Planner

The waters of the South River are open to the public for paddling, but please be aware that most of the land along the river is privately owned, so the area is best explored by boat. Because of the likelihood of encountering downed trees, the river is best paddled during times of higher water.

There are three convenient put-in points. A Wildlife Resources Commission boat landing is located southwest of the town of Garland. You can put in at the US 701 bridge (Sloans Bridge) and paddle 8.2 miles downstream to the NC 41 bridge. A second access point is at the NC 41 bridge (east of Smith's Crossroads); put in there and paddle about 8.6 miles to the wildlife access area at

Bladen County SR 1007 (Ennis Bridge). A third access point is at the wildlife access area at Ennis Bridge; from there, you can paddle 11.8 miles to the SR 1550 bridge on the Black River at Ranking Street near NC 210.

## Ownership/Access

The Nature Conservancy
4705 University Drive, Suite 290
Durham, NC 27707
(919) 403-8558
www.nature.org/northcarolina

The N.C. Coastal Land Trust
131 Racine Drive, Suite 101
Wilmington, NC 28403
(910) 790-4524
www.coastallandtrust.org

## Features

The oldest known trees east of the Rocky Mountains can be found on this meandering blackwater stream in the southeastern part of the state: a stand of 1,700-year-old bald cypress. These ancient trees are easily recognized by their huge buttresses and flat tops that have been blown out by countless storms.

The river flows 66 miles through portions of Sampson, Pender, and Bladen Counties before emptying into the Cape Fear River 14 miles above Wilmington. Water ash and cat-briar form a subcanopy of dense thickets along the banks of the river. Elsewhere along the river, slight variations in elevation allow for changes in the forest from black gum and tupelo gum in lower areas, to water hickory, American elm, and some oak species on the ridges. In a few places, dry upland bluffs along the river support longleaf pines and turkey oaks.

In recognition of the fact that the Black River is one of the cleanest waterways in North Carolina, the state designated the river an Outstanding Resource Water in 1994. The river is home to rare fish species such as the Santee chub and broadtail madtom and numerous rare mussels like the Cape Fear spike. Many wildlife species inhabit the river's floodplain, including bobcat, river otter, black bear, and neotropical songbirds like the prothonotary warbler and yellow-throated vireo.

**Bladen, Pender, & Sampson Counties**
**7,085 acres**

The Black River is a treat to canoe throughout the seasons. You will relish drifting down the slow-moving tea-colored stream flanked by stately bald cypress draped with Spanish moss. Swamp roses bloom in the spring and spider lilies grace the water in the summer. Spring is a great time to see migratory songbirds nesting, while the foliage is outstanding in the fall.

## Conservation Highlights:

By working with many local landowners and companies, The Nature Conservancy has purchased critical sections of the floodplain and acquired conservation easements on privately owned natural areas. Conservancy stewards are working to restore the upland pine plantations to longleaf pine forests. In 1998, The Nature Conservancy acquired 2,757-acre Roan Island on behalf of the Wildlife Resources Commission. This remote island is located at the confluence of the Black and Cape Fear Rivers, roughly 12 miles northwest of Wilmington, and is only accessible by boat.

## Trip Planner

All of the land along the river is privately owned and very swampy, so we advise people to visit the river on day canoe trips. Water levels fluctuate significantly during the year. You may have to maneuver and/or portage around fallen logs and trees in the river during dry periods, especially during the summer.

Following the Pender County/Bladen County line, the Black River is easy to see on a map. Some of the old-growth bald cypress can be seen from the NC 53 bridge four miles south of Atkinson. There are no public campgrounds on the river.

Several put-ins and boat landings provide access to some of the most scenic parts of the river:

- The N.C. Wildlife Resources Commission has two public boat landings on the river: one is located approximately five miles north of Beatty's Bridge on Ivanhoe Road (SR 1550 in Bladen County and SR 1201, Pender County), and the other is located 1.2 miles east of the 11/53 bridge off Long View Road (SR 1547).

- You can access the river fairly easily from either side of Beatty's Bridge. There is a sandy bank under the bridge that provides good canoe access.

- You can access the river by canoe from the NC 11/53 Bridge located just outside of Atkinson.

Here are a few options for a daylong boat trip on the Black River:

- Put in at the Wildlife Resources Commission public landing approximately five miles north of Beatty's Bridge on Ivanhoe Road and take out at Beatty's Bridge. This stretch is about nine river miles and passes through some bottomland hardwood areas as well as cypress swamp. You can park a car on the side of the road at Beatty's Bridge.

- If you are ambitious, you could put in early in the morning at Beatty's Bridge and canoe about 14 miles to another Wildlife Commission public boat landing that is about one and a half miles south of the 11/53 bridge just outside of Atkinson off NC 3. This stretch of the river contains Larkin's Cove and Three Sisters, sites where the oldest known stands of bald cypress have been found.

- Another option is to park and put in at the second Wildlife Resources Commission landing and canoe upstream toward Three Sisters. This is a nice area because it contains several coves with ancient cypress.

(Jodie LaPoint)

### Ownership/Access

North Carolina Chapter Office
The Nature Conservancy
4705 University Drive, Suite 290
Durham, NC 27707
(919) 403-8558
www.nature.org/northcarolina

THE CAPE FEAR RIVER SYSTEM IS THE LARGEST IN THE STATE, WITH TRIBUTARIES IN 29 COUNTIES. It begins north of Greensboro with the Deep River and Haw River. Near Moncure, the Haw and Deep combine to form the Cape Fear River, which flows southeast toward the coast, meeting up with the Black River about 15 miles above Wilmington. At Wilmington, it is joined by the Northeast Cape Fear River.

The river basin is 200 miles long and spans 9,000 square miles of the state. The estuarine area from Wilmington to Southport is an important habitat for saltwater animals, providing nursery space for young shrimp, crab, and a variety of finfish.

The Cape Fear is North Carolina's most industrialized river, with 27 percent of the state's population living in its basin. It encompasses a fast-growing area of North Carolina; according to the United States Census Bureau, its population increased by 24 percent between 1990 and 2000.

Dragonfly on lily pads (Ida Phillips) Cape Fear River (Richard Butner)

# horseshoe lake

## Features

A visitor to the Horseshoe Lake natural area, one of the country's most extensive Carolina bay complexes, will be rewarded with many sights that are uncommon in North Carolina. You might see an anhinga perched in a tree, black and white wings spread wide, or thousands of yellow pitcher plants floating on soggy vegetation rafts in the middle of the bay.

The largest Carolina bay in the area is called Horseshoe Lake (for its shape) or Suggs Millpond, and is best explored by small boat. This expansive, partially water-filled bay is dominated by unusual vegetation, such as floating and rooted aquatic plant beds, floating bog mats, and pond cypress stands that may have been created naturally after deep peat fires or possibly developed from beaver ponds. The lands surrounding the bay contain other rare natural communities, including pocosin, Atlantic white cedar forest, and pond pine woodland. The rim of the bay is characterized by pine flatwood, sandhills scrub communities, and an array of rare plants, including populations of Venus flytrap, white wicky, and threadleaf sundew. In addition to the rare anhinga, Horseshoe Lake is home to waterfowl, American alligator, fox squirrel, and pine barrens treefrog, as well as mammals such as black bear and bobcat that require large expanses of land.

## Conservation Highlights:

In 1998, the State of North Carolina purchased approximately 8,000 acres of the Horseshoe Lake natural area in Bladen and Cumberland Counties from Canal Industries, Inc. The tract is now managed by the N.C. Wildlife Resources Commission as the Bladen County Game Land and is open to the public for hiking, fishing, boating, birding, and special permit hunting. The Nature Conservancy assisted the state with the acquisition of the Horseshoe Lake property. In addition, Dohn Broadwell donated a conservation easement to The Nature Conservancy that protects 1,770 acres adjacent to the game land.

## Trip Planner

This area has multiple uses, including hunting. Downloadable maps of the game land and hunting schedules are available on the Wildlife Resources Commission web site.

Horseshoe Lake is located near other ecologically significant state-owned land including Jones Lake State Park, Bushy Lake State Natural Area, and Bladen Lakes State Forest. These natural areas comprise a vast expanse of unique natural communities considered nationally significant by the N.C. Natural Heritage Program.

Heading south from Fayetteville on I-95, take exit 49 and go east on NC 53/210. Follow NC 53 after it splits to the right from NC 210 after about 2.8 miles. After about eight miles

Horseshoe Lake (Mengchi Ho)

turn left onto SR 1327 just past the community of Jerome. Take the right fork when SR 1327 seems to split where the pavement ends; this is still SR 1327. After about four miles, look for a dirt road to the left. Take that road to get to the game land. Look for Wildlife Commission signs.

## Ownership/Access

N.C. Wildlife Resources Commission
1 (800) 662-7137
www.ncwildlife.org

# green swamp

Green Swamp Preserve limesink (Debbie Crane)

IN THE FAR SOUTHEASTERN PART OF NORTH CAROLINA, THE GREEN SWAMP AREA IS THE CENTER OF AN EXCEPTIONALLY RICH ASSEMBLY OF PLANT LIFE, INCLUDING CARNIVOROUS PLANTS SUCH AS THE VENUS FLYTRAP.

Featuring a complex of longleaf pine savannas and limesink ponds bound together by thousands of acres of pocosin (a type of evergreen shrub bog), the area is home to more than 400 vascular plant species and provides habitat for animals such as the red-cockaded woodpecker and black bear.

The life cycles of many plants and animals found here are tied to fire. Longleaf pine trees, for example, need fire to clear the ground for germination and to reduce competition. The Nature Conservancy actively works to maintain ecosystem health by setting controlled burns in longleaf and pocosin communities and by planting native longleaf pine trees in former commercial pine plantation areas.

Yellow pitcher plants (Ida Phillips)

# old dock savanna preserve

**Columbus County • 230 acres**

## Features

Old Dock Savanna is a unique wet longleaf pine savanna underlain with marl. Typical pine savannas have a low pH and are very acidic, whereas marl-influenced savannas like Old Dock have a higher—or sweeter—pH. Called marl savannas, these rich plant areas have an infusion of nutrients not available in more acidic habitats. There are two known areas of marl savannas in North Carolina: the Maple Hill area along the Pender/Onslow County line and the Old Dock area along the Columbus/Brunswick County line.

The savanna at Old Dock is dominated by pond pine, with an open shrub layer of titi, black gum, myrtle-leaf holly, and bayberry. Scattered among the shrubs are dense patches of herbs, including a diverse assemblage of carnivorous plants such as Venus flytrap, grasses, sedges, and wildflowers. The preserve harbors 17 rare plant species, such as the globally rare Carolina grass-of-Parnassus, savanna cowbane, and wireleaf dropseed.

## Conservation Highlights

In 1994, Mrs. Pauline Johnson generously donated a 50-acre portion of Old Dock Savanna to The Nature Conservancy in memory of her parents, Roy and Ethel Suggs. In 1996, The Nature Conservancy purchased additional land at the preserve. Historically, natural fires have kept these areas relatively open and released nutrients into the soil. The North Carolina Chapter seeks to mimic these natural events by setting controlled burns during the growing season.

## Trip Planner

This Nature Conservancy preserve is only accessible through the North Carolina Chapter's field trip program. Contact the North Carolina Chapter at (919) 403-8558 for details.

Carolina grass-of-Parnassus (Angie Carl)

Venus flytrap (The Nature Conservancy)

## Ownership/Access

North Carolina Chapter Office
The Nature Conservancy
4705 University Drive, Suite 290
Durham, NC 27707
(919) 403-8558
www.nature.org/northcarolina

# myrtle head savanna preserve

## Features

Myrtle Head Savanna is a healthy example of one of the most endangered communities in the Southeast, a very wet, loamy longleaf pine savanna. The fine sandy loam underlying the preserve is derived in part from an underlying layer of marl and remains wet or saturated for much of the year. Marl is a fossil-rich, relatively soft sedimentary rock with properties similar to limestone. It "sweetens" the soil above by lowering acidity, adding calcium and other minerals, and decomposes to dense, sticky clay. The savanna community here comprises an open pine canopy with scattered longleaf and pond pines. Pond cypress and swamp tupelo grow in swampy depressions in the preserve.

Although the savanna is very small, it accounts for a large number of rare plant species—19 have been documented here. The preserve is home to the largest known population of Cooley's meadowrue, a federally listed endangered plant species, which is one of the rarest plants in the eastern United States. Cooley's meadowrue is a member of the buttercup family; it sends out tiny pastel blooms in June. But for one small population in Florida it is found only in southeastern North Carolina and is confined to sites where marl lies near the soil surface. Cooley's meadowrue is fire-dependent. Without fire disturbance, other plants species soon take over its environment, outcompeting Cooley's meadowrue for limited nutrients and sunlight. Fire suppression has seriously affected Cooley's meadowrue habitat. The savanna also contains one of the largest known populations of wireleaf dropseed, which is listed as a threatened species in North Carolina.

## Conservation Highlights

The Nature Conservancy purchased Myrtle Head Savanna from Georgia-Pacific Corporation in 1990.

## Trip Planner

This Nature Conservancy preserve is only accessible through the North Carolina Chapter's field trip program. Call (910) 395-5000 for details.

## Ownership/Access

The Nature Conservancy
Southeast Coastal Plain Office
131 Racine Drive, Suite 101
Box Number 5
Wilmington, NC 28403
(910) 395-5000
www.nature.org/northcarolina

Cooley's meadow rue (Richard LeBlond)

# lake waccamaw state park

**Columbus County • 1,732 acres**

## Features

The primary headwater for the Waccamaw River, Lake Waccamaw has the distinction of being the largest water-filled Carolina bay in North Carolina. The upper Waccamaw River swamp is one of the largest swamp expanses in the state.

According to the North Carolina Natural Heritage Program, the lake is home to the largest group of endemic animals in the state. There are eight species that occur only in the lake or its adjacent waters. They include the Waccamaw silverside, Carolina pygmy sunfish, Waccamaw spike, Waccamaw fatmucket, Waccamaw darter, Waccamaw killifish, Waccamaw snail, and the Waccamaw siltsnail. Other rare animals include several freshwater mussels—pod lance, yellow lampmussel, eastern lampmussel, savannah lilliput, and tidewater mucket. The reason for the biodiversity is the lake's near neutral pH; other Carolina bays have a lower pH. Since Lake Waccamaw is only several thousand years old, this process of rapid evolution, called "speciation," makes it a nationally prominent area of natural diversity and scientific study.

Canoeing along the shore of this tea-colored lake will give you an opportunity to see wading birds and an occasional alligator, along with many lizards and frogs. Nuthatches, warblers, and vireos can be seen in the surrounding trees in the spring and summer. A short interpretive nature trail highlights the unique natural features of the area. A number of rare plants grow in the marshy shore, and in areas of sandhill scrub: You can find Venus-hair fern, green-fly orchid, seven-angled pipewort, narrowleaf yellow pondlily, and water arrowhead.

## Conservation Highlights

Since 1986, The Nature Conservancy has assisted the State of North Carolina in purchasing 1,338 acres of land for Lake Waccamaw State Park.

## Trip Planner

Lake Waccamaw is located 12 miles east of Whiteville and 38 miles west of Wilmington. From the town of Lake Waccamaw, head east on NC 214 and turn right on Jefferson Road (SR 1757). Go 1.3 miles and turn left on SR 1947. The park entrance is 2.6 miles ahead on the left.

## Ownership/Access

N.C. Division of Parks and Recreation
Lake Waccamaw State Park
1866 State Park Drive
Lake Waccamaw, NC 28450
(910) 646-4748
lake.waccamaw@ncmail.net
www.ncparks.gov

Alligator at sunset (Bill Lea)

# juniper creek game land

**Brunswick & Columbus Counties**
**18,341 acres**

## Features

Juniper Creek drains the Green Swamp as it flows into the Waccamaw River. Primarily surrounded by cypress-gum swamp and bottomland hardwood forest, Juniper Creek supports several smaller longleaf savanna natural areas that provide habitat for a variety of rare plants. This region also provides excellent habitat for animals including the fox squirrel, and potential habitat for the endangered red-cockaded woodpecker. The game land provides an important natural corridor between the Conservancy's Green Swamp Preserve and the Waccamaw River.

The area includes blackwater forest natural communities such as cypress-gum swamps, peatland Atlantic white cedar forest, and bottomland hardwoods. It also includes, on an isolated rise within the swamp, an older growth loblolly pine/hardwood forest with pines up to four feet in diameter. The natural hardwood swamps and uplands are frequently flooded. Rare species, including healthy populations of several rare fish and mussels, are found in the high-quality waters of Juniper Creek. The tract contains the healthiest population of Carolina pygmy sunfish, a threatened species in North Carolina and a candidate for federal listing. This species is globally restricted to the Upper Waccamaw drainage.

Four longleaf wet savanna natural areas exist entirely within the Juniper Creek Game Land. Those savannas contain populations of the federally endangered Cooley's meadowrue, four additional plants listed as federal species of concern (including savanna indigo-bush, found only in Brunswick and Columbus Counties), and twelve species recognized as rare by the North Carolina Natural Heritage Program.

## Conservation Highlights

In 2006, The Nature Conservancy acquired nearly 220,000 acres of forest land across 10 states from International Paper Company. This was the single largest private land conservation sale in the history of the South and one of the largest in the nation.

In North Carolina, the project spanned 11 counties and encompassed 76,563 acres in four distinct landscapes: the Roanoke, Upper Tar, and Chowan Rivers in northeastern North Carolina, and Juniper Creek in the state's far southeastern tip. The Juniper Creek tract included 18,341 acres, which was transferred to the Wildlife Resources Commission.

## Trip Planner

This area has multiple uses, including hunting. Downloadable maps of the game land and hunting schedules are available on the Wildlife Resources Commission web site.

Anole (Ida Phillips)

## Ownership/Access

N.C. Wildlife Resources Commission
1 (800) 662-7137
www.ncwildlife.org

# columbus county game land

## Columbus County • 9,432 acres

Heritage Program, one of its unusual habitats is channel bars, where herbs grow that do not occur in other blackwater rivers. Those rare river bar plants include Plymouth gentian, dwarf burhead, and Harper's fringe rush.

Extensive forest communities cover the Waccamaw floodplain, including cypress-gum swamp and bottomland hardwood forests. The bottomland hardwood forests of the Waccamaw are unique in the Carolinas in containing abundant Atlantic white cedar and live oaks, along with the more typical laurel and overcup oak and loblolly pine. These forest communities provide excellent habitat for wildlife such as bobcat, river otter, and neotropical migratory songbirds.

## Conservation Highlights

The Nature Conservancy has secured 8,820 acres in five tracts along the Waccamaw River, which have been transferred to the N.C. Wildlife Resources Commission to become part of the Columbus County Game Land.

## Trip Planner

The best way to explore the Waccamaw River and its floodplain is by boat. You can access the river channel at several locations:

• From Lake Waccamaw, at the end of Waccamaw Shores Road on the southwest side of the lake.

• Juniper Creek Road, located east of Old Dock in Columbus County.

• Highway 130 at the Columbus/Brunswick county line south of Old Dock.

A 16.6 miles portion of the Waccamaw

## Features

You might say that the Waccamaw River has multiple personalities. This blackwater river originates just north of Lake Waccamaw and drains roughly 804,400 acres of Bladen, Columbus, and Brunswick Counties as it winds its way southward and empties into Winyah Bay near Georgetown, South Carolina. Below Lake Waccamaw, the river resembles a typical blackwater river as it flows through a vast, flat, low-lying swamp complex more than four miles wide, which is frequently flooded. Downstream the river assumes a different personality, with high sand banks, straight stretches alternating with narrow meandering stretches of oxbow lakes and backwater bays, a ridge-and-swale topography, oxbows, and ancient floodplain as much as two miles wide in places. Here, the river's depth and flow become more variable. These features provide clues to the river's past life.

Geologists at East Carolina University have determined that the large and complex Waccamaw floodplain was partly created by sudden surges of water from large lakes that repeatedly formed during the last ice age. These lakes were apparently located in what is now the Green Swamp.

The Waccamaw is home to numerous rare aquatic plant and animal species. Rare animals include the Carolina pygmy sunfish, broadtail madtom, and the Waccamaw crayfish. According to the North Carolina Natural

Cypress stump (Debbie Crane)

between NC 130 and NC 904 on the Brunswick/Columbus line is part of the N.C. Coastal Plain Paddle trail system. A Wildlife Commission boat landing is located at the NC 904 bridge on the Waccamaw near Pireway.

This area has multiple uses, including hunting. Downloadable maps of the game land and hunting schedules are available on the Wildlife Resources Commission web site.

## Ownership/Access

N.C. Wildlife Resources Commission
1 (800) 662-7137
www.ncwildlife.org

**Brunswick County • 17,424 acres**

## Features

The Green Swamp contains some of the country's finest examples of longleaf pine savannas. The open savannas have a diverse herb layer with many orchids and insectivorous plants. Almost 13,000 acres of the preserve, however, consist of a dense evergreen shrub bog (pocosin) dominated by gallberry, titi, and sweet bay.

Many of the plants in the Green Swamp benefit from periodic burning: pond pine's cones burst and release seeds after being exposed to very high temperatures and wiregrass flowers vigorously after a fire. Longleaf pine seeds need bare ground to germinate and plenty of sunlight to grow, typical traits of plants that evolved in a landscape with frequent fires. The grasses and sedges of the Green Swamp have roots that are protected from the hottest fires, as do the orchids and insectivorous plants.

The Green Swamp contains at least 14 different species of insectivorous plants, including extensive populations of Venus flytrap, sundew, and four species of pitcher plant. The preserve is home to many rare animals, including American alligator, fox squirrel, Henslow's sparrow, Bachman's sparrow, and Hessel's hairstreak butterfly.

One of the preserve's rarest residents is the federally listed endangered red-cockaded woodpecker. The name comes from the tiny red splotch behind the eye of the male bird.

The woodpecker prefers to nest in old-growth longleaf pines with red heart disease, since it can drill a nesting cavity in the softened core of the trees. The nesting trees are easily identified by the shiny, sticky coating of resin around the cavity that keeps eggs and young safe from predators such as ants, squirrels, and snakes. It takes between one to five years for woodpeckers to complete a nest. The birds return to the same nest year after year, as long as sap continues to flow around the opening. Since these birds are so picky about their living quarters, protecting their habitat is critical to ensuring their survival.

The Nature Conservancy's many management activities at the Green Swamp include controlled burning, installing red-cockaded woodpecker nest boxes, and restoring pine plantations to longleaf pine savanna.

## Conservation Highlights

Federal Paper Board donated 13,850 acres of this preserve to The Nature Conservancy in 1977 and an additional 2,577 acres in the late 1980s. The Nature Conservancy has since purchased additional land in the preserve. The management of the Green Swamp Preserve is supported by the Estate of Harry Patrick Gold and Erma Green Gold.

## Trip Planner

The preserve is open year round, sunup to sundown. A parking area for the Green Swamp Preserve is located 5.5 miles north of Supply on NC 211. Please note that the trails

(Debbie Crane)

into the Green Swamp are very primitive. The trails in the longleaf pine savannas have recently been overrun with foot traffic, damaging the fragile ecosystem. Part of the Green Swamp is open to hunting through the N.C. Wildlife Resources Commission's Game Land program.

## Ownership and Access

The Nature Conservancy,
Southeast Coastal Plain Office
131 Racine Drive, Suite 101
Box Number 5
Wilmington, NC 28403
(910) 395-5000
www.nature.org/northcarolina

# boiling spring lakes preserve

**Brunswick County • 6,942 acres**

## Features

Brunswick County may be well known for popular beach towns like Ocean Isle and Sunset Beach, but botanists hold North Carolina's southernmost county in high regard for an entirely different reason— Brunswick County is home to the greatest number of rare plant species in the state.

Brunswick County is located in the heart of the Cape Fear region, which contains the richest flora along the Atlantic Coast north of Florida. The moderating effects of the Gulf Stream, the high occurrence of natural fires, the considerable amount of marl (limestone) underlying parts of the county, and the wealth of longleaf pine habitats and wetlands contribute to the region's extraordinary plant life.

The Boiling Spring Lakes wetland complex contains a fascinating cross-section of the Cape Fear region's natural communities. Though the area's dense vegetation may look foreboding, this preserve offers a rare glimpse of a vanishing landscape. Located in the town of Boiling Spring Lakes, the natural area contains a mosaic of unusual geologic features. A series of parallel ridges and swales are the remnants of an ancient dune system. A large number of Carolina bays (elliptical wetland depressions) stud the landscape. Fire-dependent natural communities, including high and low pocosins (evergreen shrub bogs) and longleaf pine savannas and flatwoods on the ridges and bay rims, form an intricate mosaic of habitats.

In an average natural area, there are 8 to 10 species of plants growing in one square meter, but in the wetlands of Boiling Spring Lakes there are several times that number. A bounty of rare flora and fauna is found in this landscape, including the federally endangered red-cockaded woodpecker, a variety of carnivorous plants, rough-leaf loosestrife, and several kinds of of orchid. The preserve contains more than 400 vascular plant species, including carnivorous plants such as the rare Venus flytrap.

Human activities, including development and road building, have fragmented the Boiling Spring Lakes natural area. Years of fire suppression have allowed woody plant growth to invade the open longleaf savannas and overtake many plant species. Conservancy land stewards are actively working to restore the Boiling Spring Lakes Preserve to its natural condition by conducting controlled burns in longleaf and pocosin communities and replanting longleaf pines. For more about controlled burns, see the final chapter of this guide, "Other Ways The Nature Conservancy Is Working."

## Conservation Highlights

Located within the limits of the town that is its namesake, the Boiling Spring Lakes Preserve encompasses half of the incorporated area of the town. The establishment of the Boiling Spring Lakes Preserve is the result of a collaborative partnership between the North Carolina Department of Agriculture and Consumer Services' Plant Conservation

Pleea (Debbie Crane)

Program, The Nature Conservancy, the City of Boiling Spring Lakes, and the North Carolina Natural Heritage Program.

## Trip Planner

The preserve is open year-round, from sunup to sundown.

The Boiling Spring Lakes Nature Trail allows visitors to walk through a portion of the more than 6,000 fragile acres that make up the preserve.

If you're spending time at the Brunswick or New Hanover beaches, Boiling Spring Lakes Nature Trail offers an interesting break from sand and waves. The trailhead is at the City of Boiling Spring Lakes Community Center. From Wilmington, take US 17 South to US 87 South and follow the signs for the City of Boiling Spring Lakes Community Center.

From South Brunswick beaches, take US 17 North to US 87 North and follow the signs for the City of Boiling Spring Lakes Community Center.

## Ownership/Access

Owner:
Plant Conservation Program
N.C. Dept. of Agriculture and Consumer Services
Plant Protection Section
P.O. Box 27647
Raleigh, NC 27611
(919) 733-3610

Manager:
The Nature Conservancy
Southeast Coastal Plain Office
131 Racine Drive, Suite 101
Box Number 5
Wilmington, NC 28403
(910) 395-5000
www.nature.org/northcarolina

# onslow bight

*Iris verna* (The Nature Conservancy)

The Onslow Bight extends from the lower Northeast Cape Fear River to the Pamlico River, and from offshore waters to approximately 30 miles inland.

A "bight" is a long, gradual curve or bend in a shoreline. The Onslow Bight area is a unique landform of barrier islands, marshes, riverine wetlands, pocosins, longleaf pine savannas, and many other coastal ecosystems. The landscape has some of the richest biodiversity found anywhere in the world.

These diverse natural communities provide habitat for numerous rare plant and animal species, including several species that are found nowhere else in the world. The pocosins and longleaf pine forests are critical habitat for nesting and foraging red-cockaded woodpeckers, while the delicate barrier islands are essential habitat for sea turtle and water bird nesting.

The natural communities of Onslow Bight are threatened by rapid development, fire suppression in fire-dependent ecosystems, nonnative invasive species, hydraulic alteration, and poaching of marketable species (such as the Venus flytrap).

The Nature Conservancy works with partners ranging from private landowners and local communities to the U.S. military and a host of state agencies to protect the natural treasures of this extraordinary landscape.

(Mark Daniels)

**Pender County • 250 acres**

## Features

Longleaf pine once reigned supreme on the southeastern and Gulf coasts of the United States. Before Europeans arrived, longleaf pine forests covered 90 million acres. Today, there are fewer than five million acres of longleaf pine left from Virginia south to Florida and west into eastern Texas. In North Carolina, longleaf pines covered a third of the state; today they span a fraction of their original acreage.

Longleaf pine is one of many species that need fire for survival. Native Americans set fires to keep the longleaf pine habitat healthy; so did early European settlers. Both allowed natural fires, usually caused by lightning strikes, to burn—ensuring longleaf pine health. In the 1930s, national forestry leaders embraced the policy that fire was bad and forest fires should be suppressed, not encouraged. Fire suppression dramatically affected longleaf pine habitat. Loss of longleaf pine habitat led to a severe reduction in the number of red-cockaded woodpeckers, which live almost exclusively in living longleaf pine. The species was declared endangered in 1970.

The Nature Conservancy routinely sets controlled burns at the Angola Creek Flatwoods Preserve to restore and preserve longleaf habitat. As a result, visitors to the preserve can see the beautiful stands of healthy longleaf pine and other plants such as the Venus flytrap and Carolina goldenrod, which are also fire-dependent.

Longleaf pines communities are associated with 239 rare plant and 31 rare animal species; by far the highest number of rare species associated with any ecosystem type in the state. A walk through the Angola Creek Flatwoods Preserve is a step back in time to when longleaf pine was the predominant tree in the coastal plain and a multitude of plants and animals lived in and around the majestic trees.

## Conservation Highlights

Angola Creek Preserve was created in the mid-1980s, when the Conservancy purchased and received gifts of land totaling 250 acres.

## Trip Planner

This Nature Conservancy preserve is only accessible through the North Carolina Chapter's field trip program. Call (910) 395-5000 for details.

## Ownership/Access

The Nature Conservancy
Southeast Coastal Plain Office
131 Racine Drive, Suite 101
Box Number 5
Wilmington, NC 28403
(910) 395-5000
www.nature.org/northcarolina

Angola Creek Flatwoods Preserve (The Nature Conservancy)

# shaken creek savanna preserve

**Pender County • 6,054 acres**

## Features

Few places in North Carolina remain truly natural, in a condition similar to that encountered by the first Europeans to move inland from the coast. The Shaken Creek Preserve is one of the best such natural areas existing today on the entire Atlantic seaboard, a unique home to many rare plants and animals. The landscape is crisscrossed by narrow blackwater creeks that naturally widen in spots to form flat, still lakes. Grassy openings, filled with pitcher plants, flytraps and orchids, are ringed by pine forests and pocosins that provide habitat for red-cockaded woodpeckers and migrant songbirds. White-tailed deer and black bear flourish here. Alligators are also occasional inhabitants.

According to the North Carolina Natural Heritage Program, Shaken Creek is the "most biologically diverse savanna community site along the eastern seaboard of North America." It is the only known site in the state providing habitat for four federally endangered species—red-cockaded woodpecker, Cooley's meadowrue, golden sedge, and rough-leaf loosestrife.

The Shaken Creek Savanna Preserve is also the only site where four of the five types of pine savanna are found together, including the rare Pleea flat and "very wet loamy" types. Natural communities receive a ranking based on their rarity. Both of these pine savanna types receive a "one" ranking, which means that there are five or fewer such occurrences in the world.

While Shaken Creek Savanna is a treasure in its own right, its location is equally important, sitting as it does in the midst of one of The Nature Conservancy's highest conservation priorities, the Onslow Bight landscape. Shaken Creek is situated between two vast protected areas: 100,000 acres at the Holly Shelter and Angola Bay Game Lands, which the Conservancy played a large part in preserving, and more than 150,000 acres at the Camp Lejeune Marine Base. Linking existing natural areas is critical to the Conservancy's mission because it gives species mobility, provides a buffer for sensitive plant and animal communities, and bolsters the long-term health of the landscape.

## Conservation Highlights

The Conservancy acquired several tracts of land between 2005 and 2008 from members of a hunt club who retain the right to hunt on the property. The Nature Conservancy is working to restore, steward, and monitor the preserve through efforts such as controlled burning, which this naturally fire-dependent landscape needs in order to thrive.

## Trip Planner

This Nature Conservancy preserve is only accessible through the North Carolina Chapter's field trip program. Contact the North Carolina Chapter at (919) 403-8558 for details.

Shaken Creek (Jodie LaPoint)

## Ownership/Access

The Nature Conservancy
North Carolina Chapter
4705 University Drive, Suite 290
Durham, NC 27707
(919) 403-8558
www.nature.org/northcarolina

## Features

Pender County contains some of the most biologically significant land along the entire U.S. Atlantic Coast. It ranks fourth among the state's 100 counties for its total number of rare plants and animal species. Much of this biological cornucopia is centered around the Holly Shelter region. It includes one of the largest and most significant areas of pine flatwoods, savannas, and pocosin. One of the Southeast's largest peat-filled pocosin basins comprises about 75 percent of the game land, while a 5,000-acre longleaf pine community complex is considered one of the region's most significant natural features.

The Southwest Ridge Savanna is an elongated sand ridge that once formed the southern rim of a large but now barely discernible Carolina bay. The ridge rises 15 feet above an adjacent pocosin habitat. Pine flatwoods form a sparse canopy on the ridge. Many canopy trees were destroyed in a 1986 fire. The fire, however, rejuvenated the ground cover, which is dominated by wiregrass. Seven rare plant species, including Venus flytrap and rough-leaf loosestrife, grow alongside more common plants such as creeping blueberry and bracken fern.

A portion of Holly Shelter Game Land is known as Bear Garden. It gets its name for a good reason, as there is a thriving black bear population in the area's pine forest and pocosin habitats.

## Pender County • 75,120 acres

## Conservation Highlights

In May 2002, The Nature Conservancy purchased several tracts totaling 38,320 acres from International Paper for $24 million. Two of the tracts in that purchase, totaling close to 29,216 acres at Angola Bay and Bear Garden, were transferred to the Wildlife Resources Commission for inclusion in the Angola Bay and Holly Shelter Game Lands.

## Trip Planner

This area has multiple uses, including hunting. Roads in the game lands are only open during hunting season, so please heed the hunting schedule if you are a nonhunter! During other times of the year you can park outside the gates and walk into the game lands.

Two access points into Holly Shelter offer hikers and birders a chance to enjoy some of this game land's diverse habitats. Take NC 210 east from I-40 and cross the Northeast Cape Fear River. Drive less than a mile past the river and turn left on Shaw Highway (SR 1520). Go 7.3 miles to the Wildlife Commission boat access area by the river. Follow the trail along the dike between the river and the swamp forest. Approximately one-quarter mile north of the boat access is the north entrance to Lodge Road on the right or east side of Shaw Highway, and 1.7 miles further north is Bear Garden Road, on the right. From the intersection on NC 210 and US 17 in Hampstead, drive north on US 17 for 4.4 miles. Look for a Wildlife Commission sign on the left at the entrance to Lodge Road. The road is gated and closed from March 1 through August 31, but you can

Onslow Bight backwater (Mark Daniels)

walk into the game land here and walk through the flatwoods.

Angola Bay Game Land is also open to the public, but it is more a hunting than a nature-watching area.

Downloadable maps of the game land and hunting schedules are available on the Wildlife Resources Commission web site.

**Ownership/Access**

N.C. Wildlife Resources Commission
1 (800) 662-7137
www.ncwildlife.org

**Carteret County • 2,675 acres**

## Features

This string of small islands is located across Taylor's Creek from historic Beaufort, on the sound side of Shackleford Banks. A half-mile interpretive trail on the west side of the Rachel Carson Reserve highlights the area's common species and special features. The trail meanders through mudflats, uplands, and salt marshes, illustrating the various unique environments found in estuarine systems. A small herd of feral horses roams the islands, and over 200 bird species have been recorded here. Late summer through winter offers great birding for seabirds, shorebirds, marsh birds, and wading birds, including piping plovers, oystercatchers, and terns.

## Conservation Highlights

The Rachel Carson Reserve is part of North Carolina's Coastal Reserve system, a program managed by the Division of Coastal Management to ensure the preservation of natural resources and threatened habitat in North Carolina's 20 coastal counties. The sanctuary is also part of the N.C. National Estuarine Research Reserve. In the late 1970s the Conservancy protected 398 acres of Carrot Island to keep threatened wetland habitat from being developed.

## Trip Planner

The only access to the reserve is by boat. You may go on a guided tour of the islands from the N.C. Maritime Museum on Beaufort's Front Street, take a private ferry, or kayak out on your own steam. It is only about a hundred yards across the narrow channel to the reserve. A free reserve trail guide can be obtained from the reserve office in Beaufort. Please note that bird-nesting areas and horse watering holes are off-limits to the public.

There is water access from downtown Beaufort, reached by US 70. A public boat ramp with a parking lot and restrooms is located two miles east of downtown on Front Street.

Reeds and water (Marge Limbert)

### Ownership/Access

N.C. Division of Coastal Management
101 Pivers Island Road
Beaufort, NC 28516
(252) 838-0883
www.nccoastalreserve.net

Pine Barren gentian (Debbie Crane)

**Carteret County • 14,482 acres**

## Features

Cedar Island is an estuarine barrier island at the southern end of the Pamlico Sound with many of the characteristics of an ocean front barrier island. Cedar Island is the only barrier island in North Carolina that faces inward toward Pamlico Sound. The wildlife refuge contains extensive salt and brackish marshes, as well as hummocks and ridges dominated by red cedar. Cedar Island also harbors well-developed wet pine flatwoods, pond pine woodland communities, and what is possibly the northernmost example of a coastal fringe sandhill.

The refuge is a great birding spot, as it is inhabited by northern harrier, merlin, and peregrine falcon, and provides breeding habitat for black rail and black duck. The ferry terminal provides excellent viewing of swallows, migrant landbirds, raptors, waterfowl, skimmers, and sandpipers.

## Conservation Highlights

Bayland Corporation donated 2,061 acres of this land to The Nature Conservancy in 1991. The Conservancy transferred the tract, containing 7.5 miles of shoreline frontage and valued at $1.5 million, to the U.S. Fish and Wildlife Service for inclusion in Cedar Island National Wildlife Refuge.

## Trip Planner

Late fall and winter are the best seasons to see migratory birds and not be bothered by voracious mosquitoes. Traveling in a canoe or kayak is a great way to explore the refuge's vast marshes and see the area's bird life.

Take US 70 and NC 12 east 45 miles from Morehead City or Beaufort to Cedar Island. The Lola Road office is open Monday through Friday, 7:30 a.m. to 4:00 p.m.; visitors are welcome. Lola Road provides a three-mile route to the bay, where there's a boat ramp. The refuge is only open during daylight hours. For more information, please call the Lola Road office at (252) 225-2511.

## Ownership/Access

U.S. Fish and Wildlife Service
38 Mattamuskeet Road
Swan Quarter, NC 27885
(252) 926-4021
mattamuskeet@fws.gov

Mallards (Bill Lea)

**Carteret County • 15,000 acres**

## Features

North Carolina's Outer Banks extend far into the Atlantic Ocean, making them vulnerable to the harsh weather systems created by the collision of the tropical Gulf Stream and the chilly Labrador Current just off Cape Hatteras. One of the state's great coastal wilderness areas is located on the Outer Banks just south of Ocracoke—Cape Lookout National Seashore, 58 miles of undeveloped barrier islands.

These narrow, low-lying islands (Portsmouth Island, Core Banks, and Shackleford Banks) are separated from the mainland by an open-water sound. The island chain is one of the few remaining examples of barrier islands that are naturally overwashed by the ocean and do not have artificial foredunes. Portsmouth Island and Core Banks have extensive beach berms and interdunal sand flats covered by grasses and shrubs. Woody vegetation is limited to small pockets. Tree-covered hummocks and salt marshes extend along the sound.

Although plant diversity is low in this stressful environment, Cape Lookout National Seashore is home to several rare plants, including the threatened sea beach amaranth. The islands provide important nesting habitat for the loggerhead sea turtle. Many shorebirds nest on the low sand flats and small islands, including North Carolina's largest nesting concentration of the federally listed threatened piping plover. Be sure to visit Portsmouth Village; once a busy little 19th-century port, this picturesque village is now a ghost town.

## Conservation Highlights

The North Carolina Chapter assisted the National Park Service in protecting 950 acres of Core Banks in 1974, thereby completing the land acquisition for Cape Lookout National Seashore.

## Trip Planner

The National Seashore office is located on the southeast end of Harkers Island. From Beaufort, take US 70 nine miles north and then east to Harkers Island Road (SR 1332). Turn right and drive almost nine miles to the national seashore headquarters.

You can get to Cape Lookout National Seashore on private concession ferries. For information about the ferry from Harker's Island to Cape Lookout and the lighthouse, call (252) 728-3907, and for the ferry from Ocracoke to Portsmouth Village, call (252) 928-4361.

For rental units, primitive camping, private ferry service for north Core Banks, contact Morris Marina Kabin Kamps & Ferry Service, 1000 Morris Marina Road, Atlantic, NC 28511, (252) 225-4261 or 1-877-956-6568.

For rental units, primitive camping, private ferry service for south Core Banks, contact the Park Service office on Harkers Island.

(Jodie LaPoint)

## Ownership/Access

U.S. National Park Service
131 Charles Street
Harkers Island, NC 28531
(252) 728-2250
www.nps.gov/calo

# bald head island

**Brunswick County • 11,193 acres**

## Features

Bald Head Island is located directly south of Wilmington where the Cape Fear River empties into the Atlantic Ocean. Bald Head and nearby islands comprise the only subtropical natural habitat in North Carolina and are home to cabbage palmetto and other more southerly species.

Rare loggerhead sea turtles nest on the beaches, while herons, egrets, and ibis breed on isolated islands and feed in the marshes. It is estimated that sea turtles have a one-in-10,000 chance of surviving to adulthood, as the hatchlings face many obstacles on their journey from the beach to the ocean, including predation by raccoons and crabs. Moonlight helps guide the hatchlings into the ocean, but on developed beaches, the tiny turtles can become confused by artificial lights and venture into the dunes instead of heading toward the sea. The Bald Head Island Conservancy is actively involved in protecting turtle nesting sites and educating visitors about the fragile ecosystems on the island. Boating and beach hiking are the easiest ways to see the various natural communities found on the island.

## Conservation Highlights

When the island began to be developed in the 1970s, The Nature Conservancy helped protect roughly 10,000 acres here: 9,000 acres of marsh and 1,000 acres of uplands, primarily beach and dunes. In the 1990s, the North Carolina Chapter assisted the state in protecting the maritime forests on Bald Head Island. The N.C. Division of Coastal Management and N.C. Division of Parks and Recreation now manage this area in cooperation with the Bald Head Island Conservancy.

## Trip Planner

For a fee, you can take a private passenger ferry from Southport on the mainland to the island. The Cape Fear River and Fort Fisher landings provide private boat access. No cars are allowed on the island, so you can bring your bike or rent a golf cart on the island.

For ferry tickets and marina-use maps, contact Bald Head Island Ferry, (910) 457-5003.

For sea turtle field trips, contact the Bald Head Island Conservancy, P.O. Box 3109, Bald Head Island, NC 28461. Information line: (910) 457-5786.

## Ownership/Access

For ferry tickets and marina-use maps, contact Bald Head Island Ferry, (910) 457-5003.

For sea turtle field trips, contact the Bald Head Island Conservancy, P.O. Box 3109, Bald Head Island, NC 28461. Information line: (910) 457-5786.

Sandpipers (Jodie LaPoint)

Woolly adelgid (Hope Larson); Treating for woolly adelgid (Christina Cheatha

## Invasive Species

From the mountains to the coast, North Carolina wild lands are threatened by invasive species—plants and insects that can wreak havoc with ecosystems they are not a traditional part of. As a visitor to public lands and preserves, you can do your part to prevent the spread of these invaders.

The Nature Conservancy is focusing its battle against invasives on a couple of fronts—directly attacking plants and insects on Nature Conservancy lands and educating the public about how to stymie the march of invasives across the landscape.

In the mountains, Conservancy staff are particularly concerned with the hemlock woolly adelgid, which is killing hemlocks across the eastern United States from northeastern Georgia to southeastern Maine and west to eastern Tennessee. The adelgid, a native of Asia accidentally transported to the United States, is a tiny aphid-like insect that feeds off hemlock trees. Within just a few years, an infested tree begins to sicken and eventually dies. There is a chemical treatment for the bug, but it has to be painstakingly applied to individual trees and reapplied on a regular basis. There is also some promise in using a bug to fight a bug—some beetles like to dine on the adelgid. In North Carolina, the Conservancy's Mountains office has also taken on an interesting ally in its work against multiflora rose, an Asian species once used as

*Phragmites australis* (Aaron McCall)

an ornamental. A herd of goats is being employed to eat that thorny plant.

All landscapes in North Carolina are threatened by one or more invasives. At Nags Head Woods, Conservancy staffers are working to remove *Phragmites australis*, a European reed that crowds out the native varieties. In the Sandhills, there's a whole laundry list of invasives, including Japanese honeysuckle and the Japanese grass *Microstegium*. So many, in fact, that the Sandhills Cooperative Weed Management Area was created.

And then there are the invasives that haven't yet created a foothold in North Carolina. Chief among those are the emerald ash borer and *Raffaelea lauricola*. The emerald ash borer is a highly destructive Chinese native that has attacked ash trees from Michigan to West Virginia. *Raffaelea lauricola* is a fungus carried by another Asian import, the redbay ambrosia beetle. It has killed redbays from Florida to South Carolina. Unlike hemlock or ash trees, many people don't readily recognize the redbay tree. But the redbay is the backbone of many southern coastal and swamp forests. In places such as Florida where the wilt has already struck, the forests are changing dramatically. Many people didn't realize how many redbays there were until large numbers fell prey to the wilt.

Visitors to North Carolina's preserves and public lands could play an unwitting role in spreading these and other invasive tree killers by moving fire wood from place to place. The emerald ash borer arrived in West Virginia when visitors brought infected wood into the New River Gorge. The redbay ambrosia beetle and its deadly fungus have also been spread through firewood movement. If you plan on building a campfire in North Carolina, don't bring firewood from another location. Local firewood should always be used, and any unused firewood should be left at the location where you found it. You might also want to familiarize yourself with the myriad of invasive species and rid your own backyard of them, helping to stop their spread.

More information on The Nature Conservancy and invasives can be found at www.nature.org/initiatives/invasivespecies/.

## Forest-Friendly Fire

Fire is not always a bad thing. In fact, some species need fire to survive. The longleaf pine ecosystem in eastern North Carolina is a good example of fire as a necessity for continued forest health.

Before European settlers moved into the southeastern Coastal Plain, fires occurred at regular intervals. These were typically low-intensity fires fueled by grass and pine straw, which kept hardwood trees at bay and

Crew member (Maura High)

allowed the longleaf pines and other species to thrive in the open. A healthy longleaf pine forest is essential for the survival of many plants and animals, including the red-cockaded woodpecker, which makes its home almost exclusively in living longleaf pines. Much of the original longleaf pine forest has been developed commercially, first for tar and timber production and farming, and more recently for roads and construction. Longleaf pine stands that escaped development became overgrown with hardwoods when forest fires were routinely suppressed. Not surprisingly, as a result of these two changes in land use, red-cockaded woodpecker numbers dropped alarmingly, leading to the 1970 listing of the species as endangered.

The mission of The Nature Conservancy is to preserve the diversity of life on Earth, and in doing so, the Conservancy will often replicate natural processes, such as fire, to bring a species back from the brink. To be able to use fire as a forest management tool to restore and enhance longleaf pine forests and other fire-dependent landscapes, The Nature Conservancy has developed an extensive national fire program, staffed with experts who know and understand fire.

These folks are in charge of controlled burns on Nature Conservancy property; they also assist with controlled burns on privately

Controlled Burn (Maura High)

or publicly owned property. Controlled burning is a science, and burns are carefully planned and conducted. TNC staff look at an area and determine if its ecology can benefit from fire. They develop a fire plan for the site that stipulates the conditions under which a fire can achieve its ecological goals, which typically are to knock back competing species like young hardwood trees and reduce the amount of dead material lying around, while allowing the fire-adapted species to flourish in the opened area. Without controlled fires, the longleaf forest would convert to hardwood, and the red-cockaded woodpecker and other species such as pond pine, pitcher plants, Venus flytrap, and the insects and animals that depend on them would gradually disappear. Suppression of healthy fire also leads to a build-up of fuel in the forest, and an

unintentional fire from something like a lightening strike could bloom into a huge conflagration that would destroy the forest and pose a threat to nearby communities.

Fire-dependent ecosystems can be found across the continent. They include oak-hickory forests in the Appalachian and Allegheny Mountains, pitch pine barrens in the Northeast, Midwest tall grass prairies, the jack pines of the Great Lakes, lodge pole pines in the Rockies, chaparral in the Southwest, Ponderosa pines in the Northwest, and Alaska's boreal forest. Without fire, none of these important ecosystems can survive, and neither can the many species that call them home. For more information on The Nature Conservancy and controlled burning, see www.nature.org/initiatives/fire.

# partners in conservation

The Nature Conservancy works closely with many partner organizations to protect land for public ownership in North Carolina, including the agencies, conservation organizations, and land trusts listed below.

## GOVERNMENT AGENCIES

N.C. Clean Water Management Trust Fund, www.cwmtf.net

N.C. Department of Agriculture and Consumer Services, Plant Protection Section, www.ncagr.com/plantindustry/plant/index.htm

N.C. Department of Environment and Natural Resources, www.enr.state.nc.us

N.C. Department of Transportation, www.ncdot.org

N.C. Division of Coastal Management, N.C. National Estuarine Research Reserve, www.nccoastalreserve.net

from left (John Warner); Alligator river kayakers (Debbie Crane)

N.C. Division of Forest Resources, www.dfr.state.nc.us

N.C. Division of Parks and Recreation (State Parks), www.ncsparks.gov

N.C. Parks and Recreation Trust Fund, www.ncparks.gov/About/grants/partf_main.php

N.C. Division of Soil and Water Conservation, www.enr.state.nc.us/dswc/

N.C. Division of Water Resources, www.ncwater.org

N.C. Natural Heritage Program, www.ncnhp.org

N.C. Natural Heritage Trust Fund, www.ncnhtf.org

N.C. Wildlife Resources Commission (N.C. Game Lands), www.ncwildlife.org

North Carolina Coastal Paddle System, www.ncsu.edu/paddletrails/

U.S. Geological Survey, Biologic Resources Division, biology.usgs.gov

Stone Mountain [The Nature Conservancy]

U.S. Department of Defense, www.defenselink.mil

U.S. Fish and Wildlife Service (National Wildlife Refuges), www.fws.gov

U.S. Forest Service (National Forests), www.fs.fed.us

## NONGOVERNMENTAL AGENCIES

Audubon North Carolina, www.ncaudubon.org

Black Family Land Trust, www.bflt.org

Blue Ridge Rural Land Trust, www.brrlt.org

Carolina Mountain Land Conservancy, www.carolinamountain.org

Catawba Lands Conservancy, www.catawbalands.org

Conservation Trust for North Carolina, www.ctnc.org

Davidson Lands Conservancy, www.davidsonlands.org

Eno River Association, www.enoriver.org

Foothills Conservancy, www.foothillsconservancy.org

High Country Conservancy, www.highcountryconservancy.org

Highlands-Cashiers Land Trust, www.ctnc.org/site/PageServer?pagename=land_highlands

Land for Tomorrow, www.landfortomorrow.org

Land Trust Alliance, www.lta.org

Land Trust for the Little Tennessee, www.ltlt.org

Land Trust for Central North Carolina, www.landtrustcnc.org

Lumber River Conservancy, www.ctnc.org/site/PageServer?pagename=land_lumber

Mountains-to-Sea Trail, www.ncmst.org

National Committee for the New River, www.ncnr.org

National Wild Turkey Federation, www.nwtf.org

Natural Areas Association, www.naturalarea.org

North Carolina Coastal Land Trust, www.coastallandtrust.org

North Carolina Conservation Network, www.ncconservationnetwork.org

North Carolina Paddle Trails Association, www.ncpaddletrails.info

North Carolina Sandhills Conservation Partnership, www.ncscp.org

North Carolina Trout Unlimited, www.nctu.org

North Carolina Rail-Trails, www.ncrail-trails.org

North Carolina Wildlife Federation, www.ncwildlifefederation.org

One North Carolina Naturally, www.onencnaturally.org

Pacolet Area Conservancy, www.pacolet.org

Piedmont Land Conservancy, www.piedmontland.org

Sandhills Area Land Trust, www.sandhillslandtrust.org

Sandhills Ecological Institute, www.sandhillsecological.org

Smith Island Land Trust (part of Bald Head Island Conservancy), www.bhic.org

Society for Conservation Biology, www.conbio.org

Southern Appalachians Highlands Conservancy, www.appalachian.org

Tar River Land Conservancy, www.tarriver.org

Triangle Greenways Council, www.trianglegreenways.org

Triangle Land Conservancy, www.tlc-nc.org

# further reading

Adams, Kevin. *North Carolina's Best Wildflower Hikes: The Mountains*. Westcliffe Publishers, 2004.

Alderfer, Jonathan. *National Geographic Field Guide to Birds: The Carolinas*. National Geographic, 2005.

Bartram, William, and Thomas P. Slaughter. *Travels and Other Writings; Travels through North and South Carolina*. Illustrated. Library of America, 1996.

Benner, Bob. *Carolina Whitewater*. 9th ed. Menasha Ridge Press, 2005.

Bernstein, Danny. *Hiking the Carolina Mountains*. Milestone Press, 2007.

Chavez, Karen. *Best Hikes with Dogs: North Carolina*. Mountaineers Books, 2007.

Daniels, Jaret C. *Butterflies of the Carolinas Field Guide*. Adventure Publications, 2004.

DeLorme. *North Carolina Atlas & Gazetteer*. DeLorme, 2006.

Dorcas, Michael E. *A Guide to the Snakes of North Carolina*. Ophidian, 2005.

Ferguson, Paul G. *Paddling Eastern North Carolina*. 2nd ed. Pocosin Press, 2007.

Frankenberg, Dirk, ed. *Exploring North Carolina's Natural Areas: Parks, Nature Preserves, and Hiking Trails*. University of North Carolina Press, 2000.

Frankenberg, Dirk. *The Nature of North Carolina's Southern Coast: Barrier Islands, Coastal Waters, and Wetlands*. University of North Carolina Press, 1997.

Fussell, John O. III. *A Birder's Guide to Coastal North Carolina*. University of North Carolina Press, 1994.

Horan, Jack. *Where Nature Reigns: The Wilderness Areas of the Southern Appalachians*. John F. Blair, 1997.

Johnson, Randy. *Hiking North Carolina: A Guide to Nearly 500 of North Carolina's Hiking Trails*. 2nd ed. Falcon, 2007.

Justice, William S., Ritchie Bell, and Anne H. Lindsey. *Wildflowers of North Carolina*. 2nd ed. University of North Carolina Press, 2005.

Lambert, Yon. *Selected Climbs in North Carolina*. Mountaineers Books, 2002.

Malec, Pam. *Guide to Sea Kayaking in North Carolina: The Best Trips from Currituck to Cape Fear*. Globe Pequot Press, 2001.

Manuel, John. *The Natural Traveler*. John F. Blair, 2003.

Martof, Bernard S. *Amphibians and Reptiles of the Carolinas and Virginia*. University of North Carolina Press, 1989.

Meyer, Peter. *Nature Guide to the Carolina Coast: Common Birds, Crabs, Shells, Fish, and Other Entities of the Coastal Environment*. Avian-Cetacean Press, 1991.

Miller, Joe. *100 Classic Hikes in North Carolina*. Mountaineers Books, 2007.

Molloy, Johnny. *The Best in Tent Camping: The Carolinas*. 2nd ed. Menasha Ridge Press, 2003.

Morris, Glenn. *North Carolina Beaches*. 3rd ed. University of North Carolina Press, 2005.

Muth, Timm. *Mountain Biking North Carolina*. 2nd ed. Falcon, 2003.

N.C. Center for Geographic Information and Analysis. *North Carolina Coastal Plain Paddle Trails Guide*. Available from www.ncsu.edu/paddletrails/.

N.C. Wildlife Resources Commission. *Hunting and Fishing Maps for North Carolina Game Lands*. Available from www.ncwildflife.org.

Palmer, William M., Alvin K. Braswell, and Renaldo Kuhler. *Reptiles of North Carolina*. University of North Carolina Press, 1995.

Phillips Lynch, Ida. *Guide to North Carolina State Parks*. Niche Publishing, 2008.

Pilkey, Orrin H., Craig A. Webb, and Deborah F. Pilkey. *The North Carolina Shore and Its Barrier Islands: Restless Rivers of Sand*. Duke University Press, 1998.

Pilkey, Orrin H., Tracy Monegan Rice, and William J. Neal. *How to Read a North Carolina Beach: Bubble Holes, Barking Sands, and Rippled Runnels*. University of North Carolina Press, 2006.

Potter, Eloise F., et al. *Birds of the Carolinas*. 2nd ed. University of North Carolina Press, 2006.

Simpson, Marcus B. *Birds of the Blue Ridge Mountains*. University of North Carolina Press, 1992.

Skeate, Stewart T. *A Nature Guide to Northwest North Carolina*. Parkway Publishers, 2006.

Stewart, Kevin G., and Mary-Russell Roberson. *Exploring the Geology of the Carolinas: A Field Guide to Favorite Places from Chimney Rock to Charleston*. University of North Carolina Press, 2007.

Tekiela, Stan. *Birds of the Carolinas Field Guide*. 2nd ed. Companion to *Birds of the Carolinas* audio CDs. Adventure Publications, 2004.

Tekiela, Stan. *Trees of the Carolinas Field Guide*. Adventure Publications, 2007.

Thompson III, Bob. *North Carolina Bird Watching: A Year-Round Guide*. Cool Springs Press, 2004.

Webster, William David. *Mammals of the Carolinas, Virginia, and Maryland*. New ed. University of North Carolina Press, 2003.

Wells, B. W. *The Natural Gardens of North Carolina*. 2nd ed. University of North Carolina Press, 2007.

# index